C000070206

NAVIES AND ARMIES

NAVIES AND ARMIES

The Anglo-Dutch Relationship in War and Peace
1688–1988

Edited by

G. J. A. RAVEN & N. A. M. RODGER

Assistant Editor

Mrs M. C. F. van Drunen

JOHN DONALD PUBLISHERS LTD
EDINBURGH

© Copyright the Editors and Contributors severally, 1990

All rights reserved. No part of this publication may be reproduced in any form or by any means without the prior permission of the publishers, John Donald Publishers Ltd., 138 St. Stephen Street, Edinburgh, EH3 5AA.

ISBN 0 85976 292 0

Typeset by Pioneer Associates, Perthshire
Printed and bound in Great Britain by
Billings and Sons Ltd., Worcester.

PREFACE

In November 1688, at the invitation of a group of English politicians, the Dutch Stadholder, William III, with a large fleet and army arrived at Torbay. From there he marched on London, and in London in due course he and his English wife Mary Stuart were crowned king and queen. Their rule was unusual in several respects, apart from the manner of its beginning. Until Queen Mary's death in 1694 they ruled as joint sovereigns, while at the same time William was the Dutch head of state, so that the three countries (the Netherlands, England and Scotland) were joined in a personal union. In spite of their competing economic interests, this union led to a close alliance against the threatening ambitions of Louis XIV of France.

The Anglo-Dutch wars of 1652–74 had been fought essentially for commercial supremacy, and the greater resources of England had left her in the dominant position. The commercial treaty of 1674, which marked the end of these wars, and an acceptance by both sides of the new situation, formed the background to the broad political alliance established by William III, and that in turn initiated a period of three hundred years, for most of which Britain and the Netherlands have been more or less closely allied.

A large number of activities were organised on both sides of the North Sea during 1988 and 1989 to commemorate the Glorious Revolution, among which were several historical conferences. This book contains the proceedings of the conference originally entitled 'Navies and Armies: Anglo-Dutch Partnership in War and Peace', held at the invitation of the British and Dutch 'William and Mary' committees at the Koninklijk Instituut voor de Marine (Royal Netherlands Naval College) in Den Helder on 16 and 17 June 1988. The conference was organised by Professor Dr J. R. Bruijn, Professor Dr G. Teitler, Drs H. L. Zwitzer and Drs G. J. A. Raven. The chairmen of the sessions were Professor Bruijn, Professor Dr A. G. H. Bachrach, Commander Dr Ph. M. Bosscher and Mr E. J. Grove. There were five Dutch and two British speakers at the conference, and all of the papers which were delivered are included here. Mr H. P. Wilmott was unfortunately unable to give his paper, and was replaced at short notice by Mr Grove.

v

The contributions fall broadly into three groups. Chapters 1 to 3 bear on the first hundred years of the alliance, two being devoted to the situation at sea, as seen from the Dutch and British points of view respectively, and one to wars on land. It emerges clearly from these papers how the declining power and influence of the Republic, and the diverging interests of the parties, progressively undermined what had originally been an alliance of equals, and eventually brought the two countries to war. After the wars of 1780–1784 and 1795–1813, however, the bonds between the two countries were re-established, and during the nineteenth century the British Navy acted in effect as a shield defending those Dutch colonies which had been returned to the Netherlands after the wars. Chapter 4 deals with this period. In the twentieth century a new situation in the Far East was created by the withdrawal of major British units and the rise of the threat from Japan, while in Europe in 1940 the Dutch navy took refuge with its British sister. But on both sides of the world the two navies were now equally dependent on the new super-power, the United States. Nevertheless Anglo-Dutch naval co-operation is very much alive, and the last, but by no means the least interesting two chapters deal with the relations between society and the armed forces in the two countries today.

The editing of this book has been the product of harmonious Anglo-Dutch co-operation. The contributors have revised their papers and assimilated points raised in discussion at the conference. The text was most efficiently typed by Mrs I. L. Drevers-Driesen and Miss D. Piepelenbosch.

The costs of translation were covered by a grant from the Stichting 1688–1988 (1688–1988 Foundation), to whom the editors express their grateful thanks.

July, 1989
G. J. A. Raven
N. A. M. Rodger

CONTENTS

page

Preface   v

Notes on the Contributors   viii

1. A Competitive Ally. The Delicate Balance of Naval Alliance
   and Maritime Competition between Great Britain and the
   Dutch Republic, 1674–1795
   E. S. van Eyck van Heslinga   1

2. The British View of the Functioning of the Anglo-Dutch
   Alliance, 1688–1795
   N. A. M. Rodger   12

3. The British and Netherlands Armies in Relation to the
   Anglo-Dutch Alliance, 1688–1795
   H. L. Zwitzer   33

4. 'A Very Unpleasant Relationship'. Trade and Strategy in the
   Eastern Seas: Anglo-Dutch Relations in the Nineteenth
   Century from a Colonial Perspective
   J. A. de Moor   49

5. Anglo-Dutch Relations, 1936–1988. Colonial and
   European Trends
   G. Teitler   70

6. A Necessary Evil. The Armed Forces and Society in
   the Netherlands
   J. C. H. Blom   84

7. The Armed Forces and Society in Britain
   E. J. Grove   105

Index   113

NOTES ON THE CONTRIBUTORS

J. C. H. Blom (born 1943) studied history in Leiden and took his doctorate in 1975 with a dissertation on *De Muiterij op De Zeven Provinciën. Reacties en gevolgen in Nederland*, second edition 1983. Together with A. C. 't Hart and I. Schöffer he was a member of the committee of inquiry concerning P. Menten, which in 1979 published its final report under the title of *De affaire-Menten 1945–1976*. Since 1983 Mr Blom has been Professor of Post-mediaeval Dutch History at the University of Amsterdam. He has published several articles, mostly on the history of the Netherlands from 1930–50 and also about the arising of the pillarization in the Netherlands.

E. S. van Eyck van Heslinga (born 1950) graduated at the University of Leiden in 1976. Since then she has been teaching maritime history there. The subject of her doctoral thesis was Dutch shipping and trade with the colonies in Asia during the period 1795–1806. Her other fields of interest include the living and working conditions of seamen in general, and Dutch shipping with the Americas and Asia during the first half of the nineteenth century.

E. J. Grove (born 1948) studied history at the University of Aberdeen, and war studies at King's College, London. He became a lecturer in the History Department of the Royal Naval College, Dartmouth, in 1971. After serving as senior lecturer for five years he was an exchange professor of history at the United States Naval Academy, Annapolis, in 1980–1. Mr Grove returned to the History Department at Dartmouth and was deputy head of strategic studies and international affairs in 1982–5. After a year as senior research officer at the Council for Arms Control, London, he is now a self-employed strategic analyst, defence consultant and author. His books include *The Royal Navy, Vanguard to Trident. British Naval Policy since 1945*, and a new edition of Sir Julian Corbett's *Some Principles of Maritime Strategy*.

J. A. de Moor (born 1953) is a researcher in the Werkgroep voor de Geschiedenis van de Europese Expansie Overzee (Centre for the

History of European Expansion), University of Leiden. He specialises in Indonesian and military history. Mr De Moor published *Nederlanders Overzee* with L. Blussé (Franeker, 1983); *Indisch Militair Tijdschrift. A Selective and Annotated Bibliography, 1870–1942* (The Hague, Leiden, 1983); *Imperialism and War. Essays on Colonial Wars in Africa and Asia* with H. L. Wesseling (Leiden, 1989), and several articles about Indonesian military history.

G. J. A. *Raven* (born 1954) studied history at the University of Leiden, majoring in socio-economic history, with maritime history and economics in addition. In 1978–9 he completed his military service as a reserve officer at the afdeling Maritieme Historie van de Marinestaf (Department of History of the Naval Staff) at The Hague, in succession to one of the members of the professional staff. In 1981 he became deputy head, and in 1984 head of the Department. His publications have been mainly concerned with the social history of the Royal Netherlands Navy. Recently he edited *De kroon op het anker. 175 jaar Koninklijke Marine* (Amsterdam, 1988), a general introduction to Dutch naval history.

N. A. M. *Rodger* (born 1949) read Modern History and subsequently took a D. Phil. at University College, Oxford. Since 1974 he has been an Assistant Keeper in the Public Record Office, London, and he is also Honorary Secretary of the Navy Records Society. His works include *The Wooden World: An Anatomy of the Georgian Navy* (London, 1986).

G. *Teitler* (born 1942) studied political and social sciences at the University of Amsterdam from 1960 until 1967. Subsequently he became a member of the faculty of that university and of the Erasmus University in Rotterdam. In 1974 he took a doctorate in social sciences with a dissertation on *De wording van het professionele officierskorps*, which was translated into English as *The Genesis of the Professional Officers' Corps* (Beverley Hills & London, 1977). Six years later he was appointed Professor of Military History and General Strategy at the *Koninklijk Instituut voor de Marine* (Royal Netherlands Naval College). In 1988 he took a doctorate of arts with a dissertation on *Anatomie van de Indische defensie. Scenario's, plannen, beleid 1892–1920.* His publications deal in particular with the Dutch and Dutch East Indies' defence policy.

H. L. Zwitzer (born 1929) studied political and social sciences at the University of Amsterdam and graduated in history at the University of Utrecht. From 1974 until 1987 he was a member of the staff of the Sectie Militaire Geschiedenis van de Landmachtstaf (Military History Section of the Royal Netherlands Army). From 1982 until 1987 he was deputy head of this section. He has published a series of articles about the military history of the former Dutch East Indies and about the Netherlands Army under the Republic of the United Netherlands.

1

A COMPETITIVE ALLY. THE DELICATE BALANCE OF NAVAL ALLIANCE AND MARITIME COMPETITION BETWEEN GREAT BRITAIN AND THE DUTCH REPUBLIC, 1674–1795

E. S. van Eyck van Heslinga

On the third day of September 1757 the ship *d'Anna & Elizabeth*, under command of Klaas Pieterse, sailed from Hellevoetsluis.[1] Her destination was the Dutch settlement of Curaçao in the West Indies. Before the next day was over *d'Anna & Elizabeth* had been stopped and searched by no less than nine different privateers. Further down the English Channel these tedious visits became less frequent, but the behaviour of the privateers went from bad to worse. The British sailors tried to steal everything they could lay their hands on. Finally, when the Dutch merchant ship entered West Indian waters in November, a British privateer forced the captain to sail to Jamaica. In January 1758 *d'Anna & Elizabeth* and her cargo were declared 'good prize' by a British prize-court.

It is hardly surprising that the owners of *d'Anna & Elizabeth*, the merchants I. and Z. Hope, from Rotterdam, were furious about this verdict. Klaas Pieterse carried the correct papers for ship and cargo. No contraband was found on board the ship. The supercargo of the *d'Anna & Elizabeth* informed her owners that the captain of the privateer, finding no legal reason for further investigation, finally had to bribe a judge of the prize-court to obtain the above-mentioned verdict.

D'Anna & Elizabeth was just one out of hundreds of similar cases. Although the Dutch were neutrals in the Seven Years' War (1756–1763), they lost ships and cargoes to the value of more than twelve million guilders during the first two years of this conflict.[2] The Dutch merchants and shipowners established that by far the greater part of the damage had been caused by warships and privateers of the Republic's ally, Great Britain. They aired their grievances to the States-General time after time, but without the desired effect. The Dutch government had to deal with this affair very cautiously. An *advys*

1

(advice) concerning an official reaction to the losses sums up exactly the dilemma of the Dutch Republic:[3] 'This navigation and business cannot compensate for the disadvantage which would be caused by a quarrel over that question with England, the Republic's most faithful ally, if we want to maintain that alliance for the future'. The status of the mercantile marine cannot be seen apart from the Anglo-Dutch naval alliance. It is my intention to show that for the Dutch, from the end of the third Anglo-Dutch War throughout the eighteenth century, the maintenance of a balance between naval alliance and maritime competition was an inevitable policy. To support my statement, I have to deal with the Dutch navy in general and the alliance of 1688–1689, and with the Dutch mercantile marine in connection with its competitor. After that I will put things together and give some illustrative examples of how the Dutch walked a tightrope over choppy seas. In the seventeenth and eighteenth century the Dutch navy was in fact an organisation made up of five fully independent institutions, the *admiraliteiten*. Each *admiraliteit* was responsible for the building, maintaining and fitting out of Dutch warships. The *admiraliteiten* had their seats in Amsterdam, Rotterdam and in the north-east of the province of Holland, alternately in Enkhuizen and Hoorn. The provinces of Zeeland and Friesland also had an *admiraliteit* each — in Middelburg and in Harlingen. I will not go into detail about the origin and early history of these *admiraliteiten*; that would be straying too far from the present subject. But I do have to explain some of the most important features of the structure of the Dutch navy concerning management and finance.

First, management. It is easy to understand that five separate admiralties in five or six different places are an impediment to the development of one national policy. The States-General appointed the members of the board of each *admiraliteit*. Half of the members came from the province itself; the rest of the seats were taken by representatives from other provinces. These admiralty-boards were quite independent in their decisions. In fact there was no central management. At the *Haagsche Besognes* — meetings of the representatives of the admiralties, which took place at irregular times — the members did no more than draft memoranda for the States-General. During the meetings of the States-General the provinces had to come to an agreement about the orders for the admiralties. When there was no stadholder the States-General decided upon the actions of the Dutch fleet, and these decisions were checked by the *raadpensionaris* (Grand Pensionary).

The five admiralties were also quite independent in their financial management. Each admiralty had its own source of income out of a part of the revenues from import and export duties: the *convooien en licenten*. These were paid along the inland frontiers as well as by the seaports on the Dutch coast. The tax officers were employed by one of the five admiralties. Besides the *convooien en licenten* Dutch shipowners and merchants paid levies, the *last- en veilgelden* — a certain percentage of the tonnage of their ships and of the value of the cargoes. The *last- en veilgelden* could be increased (and were actually increased) by the States-General with a special objective, for instance to bear the cost of extra convoys for merchant ships. The States-General controlled these extra levies themselves.

A third important part of the income of the admiralties was the money paid by the Dutch East India Company: a fixed amount to buy off all taxes and to secure naval protection for the fleet homeward bound from Asia entering European waters. There were several other less significant items such as tax revenue via the custom-houses on land and in the inland ports. Furthermore, for the building and equipping of the Dutch warships an admiralty had a right to receive a grant from the province, though they rarely got one. And lastly, an admiralty could just borrow money, but only with the permission of the States-General.

As Professor J. R. Bruijn has shown in his book about the Amsterdam Admiralty between 1713 and 1751, 67.5 per cent of its revenues derived from trade by land and by sea.[4] This means that the Dutch navy largely depended on this part of the economy.

So much for management and finance of the *admiraliteiten*; let me now continue with a short survey of Dutch naval history. After the three English wars (for English readers, the Dutch or Anglo-Dutch wars) the Dutch Republic joined in the Nine Years' War from 1688 until 1697, the War of the Spanish Succession from 1702 until 1713, the Fourth English War from 1780 until 1784, and finally, in 1795, was forced into the wars that would, in the end, destroy much of the solid base of the Dutch economy. Britain, on the other hand, was almost continually at war in the eighteenth century, mainly against France.

When William III became King of England in 1689, the States-General and the new king ratified a treaty of co-operation of the mutual fleets. This was not an original phenomenon; in 1678, four years after the Third English War, such co-operation had already been decided upon. And it was certainly not the last involving naval alliance. In 1787 Great Britain and the Dutch Republic renewed their treaty of 1689, after almost a century!

All the treaties confirming naval alliances followed the same lines: If Great Britain and the Republic were actually attacked, or when an attack was feared, each ally would immediately assist the other with a certain number of warships — ships of the line, frigates and fire ships. Both countries agreed upon a ratio of five to three: England five, the Dutch three. The ships had to be fully equipped and crewed. For thirty ships of the line — nine frigates and four fire ships — to be crewed by the Dutch Republic in 1689, 10,572 men had to be embarked.[5] Usually the Dutch navy enlisted about 3,500 men a year. At the time the general employment of seafarers in peacetime was estimated to be about 50,000. To force seamen to join the navy it was common policy to put an embargo on the mercantile marine during wartime.

When the allied fleet was in action, the Commander-in-Chief was always to be an Englishman. It is interesting to observe the opinion of our nineteenth-century naval historian, J. C. de Jonge, about this decision. He wrote: 'This item of the agreement turned out to be an important one, one that had far-reaching consequences for the honour and dignity of the State (the Dutch Republic) in general and for the glory of the Dutch navy in particular'.[6] De Jonge thought that perhaps the Dutch negotiators did not offer resistance because they realised that the British would never agree to be placed under Dutch command. He went on to say — clearly illustrating the Dutch nineteenth-century view — 'There are examples (it is common knowledge) of how the British always have judged, and still do, the events of the past in which the Dutch were under command of British officers'.[7] De Jonge suggested that an example was the action in 1596 when the combined Anglo-Dutch fleet sailed to Cadiz in Spain. To a present-day historian, almost 150 years after De Jonge wrote his book, this argument somehow does not sound very convincing. But even J. C. M. Warnsinck, a naval historian who wrote about the allied fleet of William III, before the Second World War, could not think of any other reason.[8] There was, however, a perfectly plausible explanation for the Dutch being indulgent towards the fact that the Commander-in-Chief was an Englishman. It seems that during earlier negotiations about military alliance on the Continent this issue had already been settled.[9]

But the Dutch negotiators did not easily give way when the order of voting in a council of war was at stake. For a long time they were opposed to the rather humiliating British proposal implying that the British officers — from high rank to low — were to be first to cast their votes. Finally, William III decided that nothing was to be determined officially, but that each nation would vote according to its usual practice. The English Commander-in-Chief had to be the last person to vote.

The treaty of 1689 was put into practice during the Nine Years' War and the War of the Spanish Succession. Some battles were fought against the French navy — not always successfully, but in the end the English and Dutch ships succeeded in ensuring their predominant position at sea. Most of the time ships of both nations were engaged in safely convoying their merchant ships to the Mediterranean.

After the peace of 1713 Great Britain and the Republic continued their co-operation at sea. During the first half of the eighteenth century most of the naval attention was focused on southern Europe and the Baltic. Sweden, Denmark and Russia were not only fighting their wars on land, but also at sea. Both Britain and the Republic were keen on securing safe passages for their merchant ships through the Sound. I will go into this later.

Then, in the forties of the eighteenth century the former enemies, Britain and France, clashed again. The Dutch Republic stayed out of the war, but it tried to live up to its obligations, albeit not with all its heart. After this, the unsatisfactory British performance in this war further weakened the alliance. Mutual relations became strained all the more. Several incidents concerning neutral Dutch ships transporting goods for Britain's enemy were responsible for growing tension, finally leading to the Fourth Anglo-Dutch War of 1780.

In this context it is interesting to notice that the tense situation did not prevent naval officers of both sides from associating in a friendly atmosphere. In March 1779 Captain J. H. van Kinsbergen, from his ship, the *Argo*, lying in the bay of Cadiz, reported that a party on board were celebrating the birthday of Prince William V.[10] He tells us: 'At last Englishman, Frenchman and Spaniards toasted, as generously as we ourselves did, the Prince, the Princesses and the Royal Family'. The toast was answered by a member of the crew of the *Argo*, who shouted: 'Heaven strike them all who think otherwise!' Van Kinsbergen's account shows how even French and English naval officers could mingle, although officially they were enemies. It also demonstrates the heartfelt sympathy of *Jan Maat* for the House of Orange. When the French armies invaded the Republic in 1795, several Dutch naval ships managed to escape to England at the instigation of their crews, as did the Prince of Orange himself.

In 1787, three years after the Fourth Anglo-Dutch War, a new naval alliance was formed. But the Dutch were called on to take action only in 1790. Van Kinsbergen was in command of a Dutch squadron which lay for six weeks at Spithead. The British expected a Spanish move, but apparently the Spanish government was eventually discouraged by this show of harmony.[11]

Let us now turn to the Dutch mercantile marine in the seventeenth and eighteenth century. The line of thought is roughly the same as was used for the navy — organisation, finance and finally a short survey, comparing Dutch and British developments. Dutch involvement in shipping was wide-ranging during the seventeenth and eighteenth century. We will, however, concentrate on the European mercantile marine, which was the actual backbone of the economy of the Republic. The bulk of the merchant fleet operated in the North Sea, the Baltic, the White Sea and along the Atlantic coastline of France, Spain and Portugal. Dutch overseas trade was an integrated and complementary system of buying the products of the first area and selling them in the second, and the other way round. The Mediterranean trade opened up even more opportunities for the system.

The mercantile marine knew no central organisation. Each ship was an independent company, often financed by several owners. The main reason for this was to spread the risks. This was not specifically Dutch; in other European countries shipowners worked in the same way. A great shipowner was someone who owned shares in many ships.

In general, we can say that around 1650 the Netherlands was the leading country in European trade and shipping business. One hundred and fifty years afterwards, at the end of the eighteenth century, Britain and France displaced the Republic from the top to the third place. What happened?

In a recent article by J. L. van Zanden about the economy of the Netherlands from 1650 to 1805, the author gives a statistical description of current knowledge about the Dutch economy.[12] In order to evaluate this a lot of research remains to be done. Van Zanden concludes that what seems to be economic decline, in comparison with Britain and France, is probably relative stability, or, as Johan de Vries called it, relative decline.[13] In other words, the economy of Britain and France flourished in the eighteenth century, but the Dutch stagnated. This can be demonstrated by looking at Dutch and British shipping. The rough figures of the total tonnage of both mercantile marines roughly agree with one another:[14]

British tonnage		Dutch tonnage	
1572	50,000	1567	160,000
1629	115,000	1636	310,000
1686	340,000	1670	400,000
1751	421,000	1750	365,000
1775	608,000	1780	400,000

At the end of the sixteenth and during the first half of the seventeenth century the Dutch clearly predominated, but in the second half of the seventeenth century the English mercantile marine was expanding at a great pace. In the beginning of the next century the tide turned; around 1750 the British had taken the lead. Dutch shipping remained stable.

At this point it is important to state once again that the international commerce and transport system formed the basis of the extraordinary growth of the Dutch economy in the seventeenth century. But this turned out to be a dangerously weak position for a small country deficient in its own production of raw materials. Another favourable condition was the political stability of the Dutch Republic in the seventeenth century. Merchants felt attracted to Amsterdam and a trade centre was born. But when the other European countries, Britain among them, conquered their internal political problems and offered a more stable climate, fortunes changed. Britain became a serious competitor to the Dutch Republic, and with this statement we have arrived at the title of this article — 'a competitive ally'. Great Britain was an ally, but also a danger to the very existence of the Republic. The three Anglo-Dutch Wars illustrate this perfectly. The cause of the first was the proclamation of the Navigation Acts, which were a direct attack on Dutch shipping. Most Dutch historians recognise the fact that the Dutch Republic was forced to follow a foreign policy of neutrality in order to save its profitable carrying trade as much as possible. The political implications for the Dutch government were described by A. Carter in her book *Neutrality or Commitment*.[15] The common opinion of naval historians is that the naval alliance with England was a perfect — or nearly perfect — match till 1713, the end of the War of the Spanish Succession. But for those who look more closely at the history of both navies before that date, it seems to be clear that from 1674 the

Dutch always put their trade and shipping interests first. The task of the Dutch navy was first and foremost to protect these interests. To illustrate this view I will give you three examples, one from 1678, the second from 1715 (shortly after the peace of 1713), and the third one a more general item from the seventeenth and eighteenth centuries.

In 1678 Rear-Admiral Cornelis Evertsen of the Admiralty of Zeeland was sent to London by William III to work out an agreement about naval alliance.[16] Extraordinary Ambassador C. van Beuningen was to be the actual negotiator. Charles II had first made a proposition which implied that Britain would have available for a Channel fleet fifty ships with ten fire ships and tenders; for the Mediterranean, the same number; for the West Indies, fifteen ships and two fire ships; for the Soundings and coastal waters of Ireland ten light frigates; and 'to the Norward' twenty light frigates. The King expected the Dutch to join with twenty-five ships and five fire ships in the Channel, the same in the Mediterranean, five ships in the West Indies and ten light frigates 'to the Norward'. Van Beuningen's answer was a more polite form of the rather blunt instruction of William III. The gist of it was that the Dutch could have ready eighteen ships for the Mediterranean, but none for the Channel. The reason was that they suspected Charles II of planning to invade France. The instruction said literally that the Dutch Republic could not possibly furnish ships or men for such a venture. Van Beuningen also offered to provide twenty ships for the North Sea and another fifteen to be sent to Denmark 'au secours du Roy du Danemarq et pour la sécurité du commerce dans la dit mer durant la guerre'. ('To help the Danish king and for the security of commerce in this sea during the war').

If we analyse and compare the English and Dutch propositions, the difference is clear. The English wanted a very strong fleet in the Channel and in the Mediterranean — against France. They also wanted to protect the West Indian area and Ireland, but the North Sea and the Baltic came last. The Dutch agreed with a fleet in the Mediterranean, but they absolutely refused to challenge the French by sending their warships to the Channel. What they really wanted was protection for their merchant ships sailing to the Baltic.

Van Beuningen also made a short but significant list with five major points, which were to be the main objectives of an allied fleet ranged against France.[17] The first was 'd'assurer la commerce et la navigation'. After that came the destruction of French privateers, warships, coastal towns and so on. Items on a list compiled by an English negotiator would certainly have been in a different order. From the following account we can learn how the Anglo-Dutch alliance fared in peacetime.[18]

In the spring of 1715 a Dutch and an English squadron went to the Sound. The Danish and Swedish kings were at war, and shipping through the Sound was severely hampered. Vice-Admiral Norris was Commander-in-Chief, the Dutch commander was Rear-Admiral L. de Veth, from the Admiralty of Amsterdam. During the first meeting of the two commanders it turned out that their instructions for this allied operation sharply deviated from each other. The English had orders to attack any Swedish warship they saw, but the Dutch only had permission to defend themselves and the merchant ships under their protection. This was a severe disappointment for Norris. De Veth explained to Heinsius, the Dutch Grand Pensionary, that Norris had contrived an intricate solution to the problem. When they spotted Swedish ships, in force too strong for the British squadron alone, Norris would provoke the Swedes into attacking. Then De Veth would be obliged to help his British ally. But it never happened. The Swedes seemed to have scented the danger. At last Norris and De Veth, when sailing home with hundreds of merchant ships, decided that it was better to pretend not to see Swedish warships, even if they were clearly there!

The most striking issue that demonstrates the different views of the two allies is the question of 'free trade'. This problem, which undermined the relations between the Dutch Republic and Great Britain from 1674 throughout the eighteenth century, pre-eminently demonstrates the close connection between naval alliance and maritime competition. The problem was briefly as follows. After the Third Anglo-Dutch War, England and the Republic agreed on the principle of 'free ship, free goods'. A neutral country was to be permitted to carry goods to and from a country at war. There was only one exception — contraband was strictly forbidden. The list of goods which England wanted to be proclaimed as contraband was quite long, and the Dutch always refused to agree to this list.

From 1674 onwards the Dutch Republic was very consistent in its policy of neutrality, or, if this was not attainable, with the principle of free ship, free goods. There were many ways for Dutch shipowners to change the flag of their ships to a neutral one, when the Republic happened to be at war. When in 1688–1689 Dutch negotiators could not prevent an official allied prohibition of shipping with France, this possibility turned out to be meaningless. In 1702 the States-General could again announce the principle of free ship, free goods. In the following year England and the Republic agreed on an absolute trade and shipping prohibition against France. Dutch merchants and shipowners did all they could to evade this regulation — with success.

In the book by Dr J. Th. H. Verhees-Van Meer about the privateers from Zeeland during the War of the Spanish Succession, it is interesting to read that despite the fact that privateering was in a sense an extension of naval warfare, the States-General did everything they could to curtail the Zeelanders.[19] Because the province of Zeeland actually supported the British view a peculiar situation arose. It was no longer possible to use the trade route to France. Only in the case of an official prohibition the Zeeland privateers could be successful. Eventually the States-General had their own way; one could say that the merchants and shipowners of the province of Holland won. When in 1712 the States-General negotiated for peace, a report was written proposing the opportunity of a unilateral treaty with France.[20] The conclusion reveals exactly the problem with which the Dutch Republic was to wrestle throughout the eighteenth century. Firstly, without Great Britain — without naval alliance — the Republic could not win the struggle with France. Secondly, England would certainly *de commercie geheel na sig trekken en de staat daarvan ontsetten.* (Rob the Dutch Republic completely of its commerce). The Dutch Republic could do nothing more than tack carefully between the Scylla of naval alliance and the Charybdis of maritime competition.

Acknowledgements

Thanks are due to Drs R. B. Prud'homme van Reine for his help and advice on some aspects of the naval history of the later part of the eighteenth century. I am also grateful to Mrs J. G. M. van Hille-Kabel for criticising the English text of the original lecture.

NOTES

1. Algemeen Rijksarchief, The Hague: Archieven der Admiraliteitscolleges XXXVII, Collectie Van der Heim 483a, bundel 1758, letter by I. and Z. Hope (undated).
2. *Ibid.*, Memorie van Nederlandse kooplieden 1758, unfoliated.
3. *Ibid.*, Advys (anonymous and unfoliated).
4. J. R. Bruijn, *De Admiraliteit van Amsterdam in rustige jaren, 1713–1751. Regenten en financiën, schepen en zeevarenden* (Amsterdam-Haarlem, 1970), p. 77.

5. J. C. de Jonge, *Geschiedenis van het Nederlandsche zeewezen*, 5 vols (Haarlem, 1859–1862), 2nd edn., III, p. 180.
6. *Op. cit.,* III, p. 183.
7. *Op. cit.,* III, pp. 183-4.
8. J. C. M. Warnsinck, *De vloot van den Koning-Stadhouder (1689–1690)* (Werken der Commissie voor Zeegeschiedenis II, Amsterdam, 1934).
9. Contribution to the discussion after lecture 'A competitive ally', 16 June 1988 (Symposium Navies and Armies, Den Helder). See also J. R. Bruijn 'William III and his two navies', *Notes and Records of the Royal Society of London*, 43 (1989), pp. 119–20.
10. Rijksarchief in Drente, Assen: Familie-archief Van Heiden Reinestein, 493-37, letter by J. H. van Kinsbergen to S. P. A. van Heiden Reinestein, 19 March 1779.
11. G. D. Bom Hgz., *De Vrijheid 1781–1791. Geschiedenis van een vlaggeschip* (Amsterdam, 1897), pp. 92–103.
12. J. L. van Zanden, 'De economie van Holland 1650–1805: groei of achteruitgang? Een overzicht van bronnen, problemen en resultaten', *Bijdragen en Mededelingen betreffende de Geschiedenis der Nederlanden*, 102 (1987), pp. 562–609.
13. J. de Vries, *De economische achteruitgang der Republiek in de achttiende eeuw* (Leiden, 1968), Chapter VII.
14. Van Zanden, 'De economie van Holland', p. 587.
15. A. C. Carter, *Neutrality or Commitment: The Evolution of Dutch Foreign Policy 1667–1795* (London, 1975).
16. Algemeen Rijksarchief, The Hague: Archieven der Admiraliteitscolleges XI, Collectie Evertsen 19, Instructie (undated).
17. Algemeen Rijksarchief, The Hague: Archief Staten van Holland, 2907 (2), letter C. van Beuningen to G. Fagel 17/27 February 1677/1678.
18. Rijksarchief in Zuid-Holland, The Hague: Collectie Heinsius 1928, letters by L. de Veth to A. Heinsius 15 June, 24 and 27 July 1715.
19. J. Th. H. Verhees-Van Meer, *De Zeeuwse kaapvaart tijdens de Spaanse Successieoorlog 1702–1713* (Middelburg, 1986).
20. Collectie Heinsius 2251, Report about a separate peace, 20 August 1712 (anonymous).

2

THE BRITISH VIEW OF THE FUNCTIONING OF THE ANGLO-DUTCH ALLIANCE, 1688–1795[1]

N. A. M. Rodger

We must begin any account of how the British viewed the Anglo-Dutch Alliance by recalling what was for all nations in the seventeenth century the fundamental determinant of foreign policy — religion. It was this which gave William III the throne of England and permitted him to involve his new kingdom in the war against France. Neither he nor his war were deeply popular in England, but none of that mattered as much as the preservation of the Protestant faith. 'We had the merit of maintaining our religion', as Dr Johnson put it, 'at the expence of submitting ourselves to the government of King William'.[2] But for the mass of ordinary Englishmen in 1688 the Dutch were natural allies in spite of being recent enemies: 'fellow-Protestants, old friends and outer bulwarks of our defences against Popery'.[3] As late as 1733, long after other sentiments had made themselves heard, an English pamphleteer could proclaim that 'the connexion between the fates of Great Britain, the Netherlands and the Protestant interest, is natural and inseparable: they compose a whole, each part of which is happy in proportion to its union with the whole',[4] and the Dutch felt the same way.[5]

The alliance therefore went to war in 1689, cemented by the most fundamental of common interests, as well as by the most effective means of co-ordination — a joint sovereign. Under the terms of the 1689 naval agreement England was clearly the senior partner in the war at sea, contributing five ships to every three Dutch, the combined fleet always to be commanded by the English admiral, regardless of relative seniority.[6] At the same time it was the Dutch who in some respects took the initiative. The 1689 agreement was largely drafted by the Dutch delegates,[7] and throughout King William's lifetime it was the Netherlands and the Dutch navy which often appeared as the more effective partner. Strategically and administratively, the Royal Navy was ill-prepared for war in 1689, especially for a threat from the westward, and the Dutch contribution to the fleet was indispensable.[8]

12

The States-General proved considerably more responsive to the requests of the stadholder than the English Parliament was to its new sovereign. For the 1689 season the Dutch squadron had to be financed in spite of the non-payment of £600,000 promised as the English contribution to the expenses of the previous year's invasion fleet. As late as 1701 William had to persuade the States-General to pay the English share of the agreed joint subsidy to Denmark because of the obstructiveness of the House of Commons,[9] and the substantial sums owed for Dutch troops sent to Ireland in 1689 remained a source of Dutch resentment well into the 1730s.[10] At sea the relative contributions of the two fleets were sharply illustrated by the battle of Beachy Head (Beveziers) in 1690, in which the greater part of the English ships failed to come into action, leaving Evertsen's squadron to sustain a heroic conflict against heavy odds. Thirteen Dutch ships out of twenty-two were lost, with heavy casualties.[11] In the fevered political atmosphere of the time everyone at once assumed (almost certainly wrongly) that the cause was treachery by the English admiral. The Earl of Nottingham, English Secretary of State, wrote that 'in plain termes, by all that yet appears, my Lord Torrington deserted the Dutch so shamefully that the whole squadron had been lost if some of our ships had not rescued them'.[12] Abject, indeed grovelling apologies were offered by the Queen in person to Evertsen, and to the States-General.[13] After this action the Dutch, and the Dutch navy in particular, occupied a position of moral superiority in the alliance.[14] The Dutch ships played a less notable part in the battle of Barfleur in 1692, which reversed the previous defeat and regained command of the Channel, but that victory was only possible because of the promptness with which the Dutch contingent had appeared to join the fleet, frustrating a French plan which depended on catching the allies before they had had time to concentrate.[15] In general the Dutch navy during the Nine Years' War, though in point of numbers and authority the junior partner in the combined fleets, evoked the respect and admiration of the English. So long as the King-Stadholder was alive there was little room to accuse his native land of not pulling its weight in the alliance.

The smooth working of the alliance, however, owed a good deal to William III's formidable abilities, and Louis XIV's formidable threats. When William's death removed the one, and Marlborough's victories diminished the other, the underlying tensions began to emerge, and English misconceptions about the Dutch began to undermine the alliance. All Englishmen admired and envied the Dutch for their wealth and success, and strove to imitate them. It was accepted by all that the Dutch were the richest people in the world, and in 1695 serious fears were expressed that the alliance would make England into a Dutch colony.[16] The only remedy was the careful imitation of all things Dutch, and one influential pamphlet advocated turning the streets of London into navigable canals.[17] Because the English, then and for long afterwards, held the Dutch to be infinitely wealthy, they took it for granted that the Republic could, if she wished, exert herself at sea more than she did, and tended to impute any failure to sinister motives.[18]

Englishmen, moreover, were generally ignorant of the internal politics and history of the United Provinces, and did not understand the extent to which the strategic interests of the two countries diverged. The English appreciated well enough that their new king had involved them in a costly war against the strongest power in Europe, but they generally though of it as a Dutch war, undertaken at least as much for the preservation of the United Provinces as to secure the Protestant Succession.[19] Englishmen did not realise that the interests of the Republic and of the House of Orange might differ. Throughout the eighteenth century British statesmen consistently misunderstood the strength and position of the princes of Orange. For them it was axiomatic that a stadholder represented all that was strongest, wisest, noblest — and as a natural consequence most anglophile — in Dutch politics, and it was only necessary to place a prince of the House of Orange in authority for all the ills of the Republic, and the alliance, to be cured.[20] However often cruel experience falsified this idea, it remained a guiding light to generations of British politicians for more than a century after the death of William III. It was fortified by dynastic links; like William II and William III, the future William IV married a daughter of the English king, and during the minority of William V his mother, the 'Princesse Gouvernante', was to exercise a dominant influence in Orange politics. But for most of the period from 1718, when George I seems to have thought of the marriage scheme, and especially after it actually took place in 1734, the connection served only to antagonise the ruling Republican elements in the Netherlands.[21] For the English this disloyalty to the House of Orange, and by extension to Britain, only reinforced their distaste for the men who dominated the Republic's government during the second stadholderless period. In this perspective the Regents of Holland appeared to be, not reasonable patriots concerned to safeguard the national prosperity, but selfish schemers, probably bought by the French, certainly out to profit at the expense of their country and its natural ally. Since the Republic's constitution gave Holland, and above all Amsterdam, all the preponderance that wealth could establish, the British were striving for an ideal which could only have been sustained by the combined talents of William III and Louis XIV.[22] What was more, the Admiralty of Amsterdam dominated the Republic's navy, so that it was in naval co-operation, or the lack of it, that the friction between the two countries most readily showed itself.

Moreover, the commercial rivalry which had precipitated three Anglo-Dutch wars did not dissolve in 1688, and the interests of Dutch shipowners and merchants in the European carrying trades contained as many seeds of conflict as they had done ever since the Treaty of Nonsuch in 1585. Throughout the eighteenth century the first point of friction was the Anglo-Dutch Treaty of 1674, which confirmed that free ships made free goods, and stated that only actual munitions of war could be classified as contraband. Naval stores were explicitly made free.[23] Thus, one of the most important Dutch trades was safeguarded, and one of the most important British strategic interests in a war with France was denied. There was no easy compromise available on this issue. So long as the alliance appeared for the statesmen of both nations the foundation of their foreign policy, the issue was not pressed too hard, but it remained a deep division in principle, and a matter of constant trouble in practice. At the same time it had a paradoxical effect of strengthening the alliance, for, given its rights as guaranteed by the 1674 treaty, the Republic was much less troublesome to Britain as an ally which could be pressured into supporting the common war effort, than as a neutral with untrammelled freedom to trade.[24] So long as the Republic was prepared to acknowledge the 1678 treaty of mutual assistance and go to war with Britain, its position under the 1674 treaty was basically safe, however much it might be modified under the pressure of war; once the Republic chose neutrality it became a serious question whether it might be more troublesome to Britain as a neutral than as a declared enemy.[25]

With William III dead and the main theatre of naval war shifted to the Mediterranean, the War of the Spanish Succession began to show up some of the weaknesses of naval co-operation between the allies. As early as 1689 the States-General were trying, over the strong protests of their admiral, Philips van Almonde, to get a shipment of munitions sent on board Dutch ships of the allied squadron to the Emperor of Morocco, with whom England was then at war.[26] During the next war divergent strategic interests began to be more obvious. At the operational level Anglo-Dutch relations remained good, and there were no complaints of Dutch failures in action, but it began to seem that the States-General were reluctant to support war aims which did not serve the immediate interests of the Republic, and more particularly of Holland. The numbers of Dutch ships supplied to the joint fleets consistently fell behind the quota established by treaty. In 1703 the Dutch squadron under Van Almonde arrived six months late, preventing any useful action in the Mediterranean. Moreover, he brought only twelve of the thirty-six ships promised, the others remaining in home waters under Dutch command.[27] At the same time it was generally believed that the interests of Amsterdam bankers in Spanish treasure were working (unsuccessfully, in the event) to prevent any interception of the Franco-Spanish *flota* of that year.[28] The naval agreement for the 1704 campaign was repudiated by the States-General almost as soon as it was made, and the squadron promised for the blockade of Dunkirk sailed instead to the Baltic, where it convoyed home Dutch trade before finally joining the allied squadron in July.[29] After 1705 the Dutch withdrew altogether from the Dunkirk blockade.[30] The States-General were consistently reluctant to become involved in overseas expeditions, especially in the West Indies.[31]

Immediately after the capture of Gibraltar, on the approach of the French fleet, they insisted on withdrawing six ships from Rooke's fleet, and then excused themselves with the argument that the French would never have offered battle if the combined squadron had not been sufficiently reduced first![32]

Beneath these frictions there lay, not only divergent interests, but rational disagreements on strategy. There were good, and not purely selfish reasons for Dutch warships to concentrate on convoying trade, for which they were technically better suited, being too slow, leewardly, and in many cases small, for fleet operations.[33] The Dutch preference for convoy over blockade had strong arguments in its favour.[34] But Dutch dispositions were also influenced by divisions between Holland and Zeeland. The privateers of Flushing and Middelburg shared many strategic interests with England against Holland, notably in the blockade of Dunkirk and the interdiction of trade with France, and as early as 1702 Zeeland withdrew from the Republic's naval preparations to safeguard its own interests. There were no doubt plausible reasons to do so, but 'few contemporaries in Amsterdam and the Hague, any more than in London and Vienna, were likely to view the activities of the

Admiralty at Middelburg in this charitable light'.[35] The subsequent Dutch withdrawal from the blockade of Dunkirk may not have been unrelated to Holland's resentment.[36]

A further cause of friction within the alliance was the question of seniority and chains of command. William III had insisted on the English having overall command at sea for obvious political reasons, but for equally obvious reasons it was resented by Dutch officers.[37] With rare exceptions among small squadrons, English officers always commanded whenever the two navies worked together.[38] Dutch admirals, however, loyally co-operated with their allies, and the only immediate problems arose in the higher direction of the fleets. William III's personal authority as King and Admiraal-Generaal[39] to give orders to both navies was not disputed, but who could issue orders in his absence was unclear. On at least one occasion Nottingham wrote (in Dutch) to Callenburgh, conveying the Queen's commands, but Van Almonde insisted that only an order signed by the Queen in person would suffice to alter the States-General's dispositions, and not all Dutch officers would even accept that.[40] After the death of William III the procedures for allied co-operation grew ever more cumbrous. The Dutch ships of the combined fleet were supposed to be entirely under joint command, to symbolise which they flew English jacks with their Dutch ensigns,[41] but in practice all commands had to be relayed, in the form of requests, via the Dutch minister in London. The procedure necessary to organise a local convoy may be illustrated by this letter, written in March 1711 by the Secretary of the British Admiralty to Lord Dartmouth's under-secretary:

> Having this day received a letter from Sir Edward Whitaker giving an account that the Dutch men of war at Portsmouth will be ready to proceed on their voyage the latter end of this week; my Lords Commissioners of the Admiralty desire that my Lord Dartmouth will please to move her Majesty that the envoy from the States-General may be desired, to write to the Commander-in-Chief of the Dutch ships of war aforesaid.[42]

All this cost time and patience.

So for many reasons the English became increasingly exasperated with their allies in the course of the War of the Spanish Succession, and the new Tory, and rather High-Church government, less close to the Dutch in either politics or religion, was more willing to give way to its feelings.[43] The Tories in particular became convinced that the Dutch were profiting largely from a war in which they participated only when

it suited them. In 1711 Admiral Wishart was sent to the Hague with a
final demand for effective co-operation, and after his return frustrated,[44]
the ministry finally authorised the publication of Swift's famous
pamphlet *The Conduct of the Allies*. 'No nation', wrote Swift, 'was ever
so long or so scandalously abused by the Folly, the Temerity, the
Corruption, the Ambition of its domestick enemies; or treated with so
much Insolence, Injustice and Ingratitude by its foreign friends'.

The Dutch, he maintained, 'never once furnished their Quota of
Ships or men; or if some few of their Fleet now and then appeared, it
was no more than appearing, for they immediately separated to look to
their Merchants and protect their Trade'.[45] In 1712 the House of
Commons resolved that the Dutch quotas had usually been short by
more than half, and sometimes by two-thirds — and that the Republic
owed £11,514 for naval supplies.[46] This was temperate criticism
compared with some pamphleteers. One of them ingeniously calculated
that the Dutch had made a profit on the war of £12,235,847. 5s. 5d: 'No
nation, no, not a petty Conquer'd Province, was ever treated with more
Contempt, or more infamously Bubbl'd and Amus'd, than *Great-Britain*
has been by its Al--s, especially the *D---h'*.[47] A recent historian has
argued that the United Provinces' failures to meet their naval obligations
'reflected disagreement about naval strategy rather than a reluctance to
assist England in the war effort',[48] but it certainly did not seem that
way to many Englishmen at the time. The Dutch for their part regarded
the English making a separate peace in 1712 as a gross betrayal.[49]

Further disagreement arose after the Peace of Utrecht over joint
operations in the Baltic. Neither country was directly involved in the
Northern War, but both had extensive Baltic trade to protect from the
privateers of either side. A joint squadron was therefore dispatched in
1715 with orders to convoy the trade home, but to engage in no
hostilities. Those, at least, were the orders the Dutch ships received,
and which the States-General were led to expect would be given to the
British admiral as well, but when Norris and De Veth met and showed
their orders to one another, it became clear to the Dutch that they had
been tricked into joining a squadron with far more aggressive intentions
than they liked. The protection of allied trade was a legitimate concern
of the alliance; the interests of the Elector of Hanover emphatically were
not. In the following year, by which time Hanover was actually a
belligerent, similar disagreements arose, and it was very difficult for the
Dutch ships to avoid entanglement in hostilities. Naturally the States-

General resented this manoeuvre, and George I resented their refusal to be manipulated, so allied relations declined once more.[50]

All these disagreements were built upon the continued British overestimate of what might reasonably be expected of the Republic, and of its fleet in particular.[51] Dutch naval power was in fact in steep decline, with the admiralties in a parlous financial position. In the ten years from 1714 to 1724 the fleet fell from 103 ships to 63.[52] Exhausted by the wars, with debt and taxation very high, the Republic was no longer able to play the role of a great power which Britain still expected of it.[53] In internal affairs the constitution, never very nimble, was showing an increasing tendency to sink into 'een moeras van kleine kwesties, kleine belangen, kleine intrigues', while in Holland men remarked upon the progressive disintegration of the province into 'achttien republiekjes'.[54] The views of Englishmen who had to deal with the government in the Hague were caustic: 'This State jogs along like a resty Jade, a whip and a spur make him advance a step or two, but ere you are aware, he stops short again, and all your trouble is to begin'.

'These people have all the symptoms of a crazy Government, they are jealous, peevish, complaining, wilfull, they will have everything and do nothing'.[55]

Particularly well-informed observers, like Harrington, the Secretary of State in 1741, had actually noticed that the Dutch were no longer the richest people in the world: 'The dilatory proceedings of that divided Republick . . . together with the weak and indebted state of their Government, and their great apprehensions of France and Prussia, have fully convinced the King of the slow and feeble assistance, that must be expected from thence'.[56] But most British politicians took it for granted that Dutch failures were failures of will, not of means, and as late as 1746 Chesterfield wrote to a Dutch correspondent that 'people here have no idea of the impotence of your Government, and the Dutch have no conception of the inefficiency of ours'.[57]

An alliance which was the prisoner of such destructive misunderstandings clearly had its weaknesses, but it needs to be emphasised that neither country seriously contemplated abandoning it. Indeed both felt free to grumble because the alliance seemed such a fixed and immovable pole of the diplomatic universe. For all the complaints, each party needed the other; the Dutch needed free trade at sea and support for the Barrier Treaties which guaranteed their southern frontiers; the British needed friends in Europe and support for the Protestant

Succession. Moreover, they received it, in both 1715 and 1719, when troops were promptly sent to help suppress Jacobite rebellions.[58] In 1729, when the Royal Navy mobilised against Spain, a Dutch squadron under Van Aerssen joined Wager at Spithead. This was the last occasion when the naval alliance of 1688 worked properly, and the last on which the Republic appeared as a major sea power. Its quota was filled, and the Dutch ships made a good impression.[59]

At the same time this mobilisation foreshadowed future difficulties, for in reality Dutch participation was arranged by Townshend and Van Slingelandt, not to strengthen allied sea power, but to weaken it. Alarmed by the belligerence of his colleagues, Townshend invoked Dutch involvement as the perfect means of gaining time for negotiation: Dutch participation guaranteed that all decisions would be subject to prolonged delay, and so Van Aerssen's ships served as a ball and chain to restrain the rasher members of the British administration while the negotiations proceeded.[60]

It was an apt symbol of the decline of Anglo-Dutch naval co-operation. Hitherto the British had not often complained of the efficiency of Dutch ships when the States-General chose to send them, but in the War of the Austrian Succession it was quite otherwise. The Dutch refused to be involved in the 1735 and 1739 mobilisations against Spain,[61] but in 1744 when France entered the war the Republic agreed to send a squadron of twenty ships. The request was made on 14 April, and the first six ships arrived in July. Later that month part of the squadron sailed with Sir John Balchen for the Mediterranean, but off Cape St. Vincent they abruptly withdrew, alleging lack of victuals and water, with the result that the whole Mediterranean strategy had to be abandoned.[62] The Dutch squadron was commanded by Admiral Hendrik Grave, who was 73 and had not been at sea for eighteen years. His subordinate flag-officers spent much time intriguing against him, both with the British and the Dutch authorities, and as most of the Dutch ships were in port most of the time they had ample opportunity to do so.[63] In January 1745, twelve days after Grave's squadron had at last reached its promised strength of twenty ships, he and half of it were abruptly ordered home.[64] With a Jacobite invasion imminently expected, the British viewed its departure with unfeigned anger.

The remaining ten ships were left at Spithead under Vice-Admiral Willem 't Hooft, but because of sickness, damage, and above all, shortage of victuals, they gave very little service. In May he had three ships at sea with convoys, and all the remainder disabled. By October all but six ships had returned home.[65] All orders for Dutch ships had, as before, to pass through London; they were forbidden by the States-General to put to sea except in company with British ships. The Dutch squadron was supposed to keep together as far as possible, and the system of *kostpenningen* made it unacceptable for Dutch ships to lend men to one another in order to get at least a proportion out to sea.[66] Then in November Admiral Vernon so far forgot himself as to issue a direct order to one of the Dutch ships supposedly under his command, and 't Hooft took instant umbrage, demanding his recall from the States-General.[67] In December, with the Jacobite army at Derby and French assistance imminently expected, the last Dutch ships sailed for home. The British Admiralty, with what seems in the circumstances to be some restraint, expressed 'surprise' at their leaving at this 'critical juncture'. In private they were less diplomatic.[68]

This unhappy campaign set the tone for the naval alliance for the rest of the war. Unconvinced by Dutch excuses of lack of money, the British assumed that the shortage of victuals was a device to retain Dutch ships on the coastal convoys which suited Dutch interests, if not to avoid battle altogether.[69] 't Hooft's conduct convinced Vernon, 'that he must have some secret orders from his masters, to get their ships as much as he can out of the way of meeting with the French, which I think they are not like to be better than at Spithead'.[70] In the autumn of 1747 the Duke of Newcastle wrote to a colleague, 'The Dutch ships are taken from the defence of their own country against the French to convoy their trade safe into French ports, against the English privateers. Sure there was never such a conduct known'.[71] At this time, with the French on the borders of the Republic and a British squadron in the Scheldt to assist in the defence of Zeeland, the Duke of Bedford, First Lord of the Admiralty, learnt with incredulity that at the same time as he was being pressed to leave Mitchell's squadron on station to protect the Republic, the Dutch ships in the river were ordered to take refuge from the ice in British ports.[72] The British accepted all this because they had no choice: in the crisis of the Jacobite rebellion they badly needed whatever Dutch assistance they could get, while the Republic was technically not even a belligerent, and certainly not so seriously threatened. As Lord Sandwich wrote in 1746, 'I fear in our present situation their alliance is too necessary for us to suffer us to take any hasty step that may be likely to engage them in desperate destructive measures'.[73]

The presence of Commodore Mitchell's squadron in the Scheldt in

1747, together with the work of British agents and British money acting upon domestic discontents, proved to be the trigger which brought about the event which British statesmen had so long looked forward to as the cure for all the ills of the alliance — the restoration of the stadholderate.[74] Now, with George II's son-in-law in authority in the Republic, they thought there could no longer be any obstacle to wholehearted Anglo-Dutch co-operation. The proposition was believed in quite as fervently by the Bentinck brothers, leaders of the Orange party, as by British politicians.[75] It was also believed in by Vice-Admiral Schrijver, the Orangist flag-officer who came to England in command of the Dutch squadron in 1748. As one of Grave's seconds, Schrijver had left an impression of obstructiveness, but under the new regime he was full of enthusiasm for the common cause:

> It is at present of more importance than ever for the honour of His Serene Highness the Prince of Orange and Nassau, that all possible injury be done to the enemy with the squadron of the Republic, instead of remaining in a harbour, which has hitherto been the way of direction in the Republic . . . It will also serve to convince the old administration, which is the occasion, that the squadron was not ready sooner, & acting upon the enemy a great while ago.[76]

The British were charmed:

> We had formed a wrong opinion of Admiral Schrijver while he was last with us in England: he was then discontented and uneasy on account of the bad orders he was under, and the ill condition of his ships, which he knew were kept unprovided that they might not act; and as I believe that vexation, working upon a lively disposition, made him a little imprudent in his expressions and behaviour in places where he ought to have been on his guard; but that is entirely altered: he comes now with orders and in a condition to act, and I believe I can safely say that he is one of the ablest and honestest officers in this service.[77]

All these high hopes were swiftly dispersed. William IV proved to have no magic method to restore Dutch finances, and was obliged to seek a British subsidy before he could do anything.[78] Schrijver's six ships arrived in January 1748 in need of immediate dockyard attention. They had on board the materials to make up the spars and sails they needed, but the Dutch artificers could not do the work without dockyard assistance.[79] Four different calibres of small arms had been provided, and no ball to fit any of them, so all the small shot would have to be recast, for which purpose bullet moulds were ordered from London.[80] Reluctantly Schrijver agreed to hoist a rear-admiral's flag if necessary to serve under Rear-Admiral Hawke ('een inferieur caracter'),[81] but meanwhile his ships were still disabled. Finally, Schrijver did manage to get to sea and cruise in the Western Approaches, but soon his flagship the *Haarlem* was disabled by sickness and obliged to take refuge in Lisbon.[82] A month after Schrijver's squadron reached Portsmouth a Dutch fifty-gun ship appeared from Hellevoetsluis and requested to be docked, which was done. It was then discovered that she was not part of the auxiliary squadron, was victualled only for a month and had orders to return home as soon as the dockyard had finished with her.[83]

Nothing in this campaign, or in this war, gave much comfort to the enthusiasts for the Dutch alliance, or for the virtues of the House of Orange as its natural cement. It was true that Dutch troops had been sent to England in 1745, but they earned little gratitude, being 'badly led, ill-provided and very unwilling'.[84] The Dutch retreat from the barrier fortresses in that year was widely attributed to cowardice, if not to treachery.[85] On the Dutch side all the complaints of interrupted trade, inevitable in a French war, were presented with renewed bitterness.[86] But the remarkable thing is how few people were yet ready to contemplate a change in the diplomatic universe with which they had grown up, and how many were still eager to pretend that nothing had changed in fifty years, and William IV was a worthy successor to William III. Count William Bentinck, for example, wrote to the Empress Maria Theresia in 1750 that a British minister, 'dans toute affaire du continent ne peut aller que de pair avec la République, s'il ne veut se perdre',[87] a view which was half a century out of date. There were British statesmen who wished to cut free from the alliance; the Duke of Bedford, for one, likened it to tying oneself to a dead corpse,[88] but they were still in a small minority.

Some small part of this may be attributed to continuing personal and technical contacts between the two countries, and the two navies. Although it was some time before the English realised it, the tide of technical knowledge, at least in naval affairs, began to ebb back across the North Sea almost as soon as the alliance was formed. When a joint signal book was adopted in 1689 it was the English 'Sailing and Fighting Instructions' which were chosen as the more advanced.[89] As soon as joint squadrons began to work together it became clear that Dutch ships were generally slower and more leewardly than English, and during the War of Spanish Succession in particular, there were numerous complaints from English admirals of the difficulty of keeping Dutch ships in company.[90] Under pressure from Schrijver for one, the

Amsterdam Admiralty in 1727 obtained English shipwrights to improve its designs. The *Provincie van Utrecht*, first product of the new master shipwright, Thomas Davis, was well regarded at Spithead in 1727, and his next ship, the *Westerdijkshoorn*, aroused admiration in Toulon and Genoa.[91] Even though Davis had actually come from Imperial service, and John May, his assistant, from France, the presence of English shipwrights may have done something to maintain professional contacts between the services. Few of the Dutch families that William III established in the English nobility seem to have maintained their Dutch links for long: the second Earl of Albemarle is a possible exception,[92] but his son, Admiral Keppel, seems to have had nothing Dutch about him but his name. One notable exception is Captain John Bentinck, son of Count William, who lived in Holland but made a successful career in the Royal Navy.[93] But this is an insignificant total of personal contacts, though no doubt it could be added to, and cannot account for the preservation of the alliance. Undoubtedly it survived any active enthusiasm for it because neither party had a real alternative, and because the British at least always overrated its importance, and continued to cherish the fantasy that somewhere — somewhere near the House of Orange — there was a great power lurking behind the unpromising façade of the United Provinces. For the Republic in her declining power, alliances of some sort were a necessity. As Van Slingelandt put it, 'Notre situation et notre dépendance . . . nous forceront toujours de suivre le torrent, il n'y a que les montagnards et les insulaires qui peuvent, et encore avec beacoup de peine, songer à la neutralité dans les troubles générales'.[94]

The Seven Years' War marked a further decline in the effectiveness of the alliance. In 1756, with a French invasion feared, Britain demanded the assistance specified by the treaties, and actually sent transports to Hellevoetsluis to collect them, but the Republic declined to provide the men.[95] Reluctant to become involved in a colonial war, aware that Britain could offer little protection against a serious French invasion, the Netherlands resolved to take the profits of neutrality.[96] Naturally this led rapidly to a crisis, as Britain sought to prevent her allies supporting her enemy's war effort. In spite of much provocation, however, and the enforcement of harsh wartime measures (notably the famous 'Rule of 1756') the treaties remained formally in force, and both countries exerted themselves to avoid a real rupture.[97] It was obvious by then that the 1674 treaty 'was badly in need both of revision and of explanation', but it suited neither side to renegotiate it formally, and a *modus vivendi* was worked out which preserved both English and Dutch vital interests.[98] Dutch convoys were sent out, but did not attempt to force British blockades.[99] The British devoted real efforts to eliminating justified Dutch grievances, for example, against British privateers' piracies in the Channel.[100] When Dutch ships laden with naval stores for France were stopped, no attempt was made to break the 1674 treaty by declaring them lawful prize. Instead the practice of past wars was revived, of buying their cargoes for British use — a solution tolerable for all parties, except of course the French.[101] Even a small Anglo-Dutch war in Bengal failed to disrupt the alliance fatally.[102]

So after the Seven Years' War the Anglo-Dutch Alliance continued in force, but by this time it was little more than a shell. Even token military and naval co-operation had vanished. The Scots Brigade of the Dutch army was grudgingly allowed to recruit sixteen Scotsmen in 1764, but next year it was refused permission.[103] The 'diplomatic revolution' of 1756 had made a nonsense of the barrier fortresses, and France seemed much more potent, both as enemy and friend of the Republic, than Britain.[104] The Jacobite threat had finally collapsed, and Britain's attention was turning outwards, to a colonial world where the Dutch featured only as competitors, interlopers and smugglers. The accession of George III, a monarch less concerned than his grandfather with Hanoverian interests, hastened Britain's virtual withdrawal as a European power.[105] Now the ancient alliance seemed to survive only as a means of securing to a grasping and ungrateful people privileges which they had no right to hold, and no means of preserving. The British government was determined to deny the Dutch the terms of the 1674 treaty in any future war with France.[106]

When that war came Britain's attitude towards the Netherlands had already been inflamed by the Republic's support for the American rebels. St Eustatius played a crucial role in supplying the rebellion with arms, Amsterdam in raising money.[107] The Dutch flag covered every sort of belligerent and rebel trade.[108] When John Paul Jones found refuge in the Texel relations sank lower still, and in March 1780 the British gave the Dutch three weeks to supply the succours specified in the 1678 treaty, or have the 1674 treaty abrogated. In April the States-General voted for unlimited convoy — that is, through a British blockade if necessary — and France rewarded them with the suspension of all duties on Dutch shipping. Finally, the imminent Dutch accession to the Armed Neutrality provided Britain with a reason to declare war.[109]

The decision was taken at a cabinet meeting on 16 December 1780, and by a remarkable stroke of fortune we possess an eye-witness account of the deliberations at which the solemn decision was taken to abandon Britain's second-oldest alliance, the foundation of foreign policy for a century. The meeting was held, as cabinet meetings usually were, over dinner, and as usual, foreign affairs came around with the port. So momentous was the decision to be reached that Lord North, the Prime Minister, and Lord Bathurst, Lord President of the Council, immediately fell asleep and remained so all evening. Lord Hillsborough, the Secretary of State for the Southern Department, 'nodded and dropped his hat', while Lord Sandwich, First Lord of the Admiralty, 'was overcome at first, but rubbed his eyes and seemed attentive'. Meanwhile, Lord Stormont, who as Northern Secretary was responsible for relations with the Republic, read out some papers on the subject: 'The Chancellor [Lord Thurlow] and Lord George Germain [Secretary of State for the American Department] only gave them consideration, but when the others awoke they approved of what was proposed'.[110]

It has recently been argued that the real author of the policy thus adopted by the Cabinet was Sir Joseph Yorke, the British minister in the Hague. Yorke had been at the Hague since 1751; he was a man of long experience, deep knowledge and invincible prejudice. His abrupt and brutal manner, his entire ignorance of the arts of tact and compromise, his easy assumption of vice-regal rights over the States-General and the stadholder, had long poisoned Anglo-Dutch relations. Now he determined to promote a war, not simply to eliminate the hated treaty of 1674, but to bring about a domestic revolution in the Republic. Yorke was perhaps the last true believer in the old gospel of the alliance. Long acquaintance with William V, whom he habitually treated as a delinquent child, had not shaken his faith in the House of Orange. The crisis of war had brought the Dutch to their senses in 1672 and 1747; another war should do the same for William V. 'Something of a political convulsion must happen to bring the Republic back to its true and only system'.[111]

In fact, of course, the political convulsion the war promoted was the rise of the Patriots, an event not intended, or anticipated, by Sir Joseph Yorke. This in turn led to the 1787 Anglo-Prussian coup, which did indeed install a sort of ghostly revival of the old order, complete with Anglo-Dutch naval co-operation.[112] In the Nootka Sound crisis of 1790, Van Kinsbergen brought a Dutch squadron to Spithead to join the combined fleet against Spain much as Van Aerssen had done sixty years before.[113] By this time, however, Dutch squadrons had long ceased to have more than a token value to Britain. What still mattered were contacts and possessions. Van Kinsbergen, for example, having served in the Russian navy, was able to advise Pitt during the Ochakov crisis.[114] In the Far East the Dutch remained formidable colonial rivals with whom the British wished to reach an accommodation, while the Dutch bases at Trincomalee and the Cape figured increasingly in British calculations as the keys to India. Fear that they might fall into French hands was a strong influence on British policy both in 1787 and again in the 1790s.[115]

After more than a century, the naval alliance forged in 1688 was briefly and artificially revived in the utterly different world of the 1790s, only to perish for good in the tumult of the French Revolution. It never reconciled the divergent interests of the two countries, and in the end it did not survive the great discrepancy which developed in their power as well as their policies, but on the practical level of naval co-operation it worked much better than on the theoretical level of national interests. Even in the 1740s, when the ineffectiveness of the Dutch squadron aroused fury and alarm, personal relations between Dutch and British officers (the abrasive Schrijver sometimes excepted) remained good — often better than those between Dutch officers — and the two navies built a tradition of joint operations which survived even the *Franse tijd*. Virtually every generation of Dutch officers, from 1688 to the nineteenth century, contained some who had served with the British, and that connection survived all the vicissitudes of the Anglo-Dutch Alliance. There is no doubt that the alliance was bedevilled throughout by the ignorance and unrealistic expectations of British politicians, but it worked as well as it did at sea, chiefly thanks to the officers of both navies.

NOTES

1. In preparing this paper I have been greatly helped by colleagues who know much more about Dutch, and diplomatic, history than I do, notably Dr J. Black, Dr Ph. M. Bosscher, Professor J. R. Bruijn and Dr H. M. Scott.
2. J. Boswell, *The Life of Samuel Johnson*, ed. R. W. Chapman (London, 1953), p. 611.
3. J. R. Jones, 'English Attitudes to Europe in the Seventeenth Century', in J. S. Bromley and E. H. Kossman, eds, *Britain and the Netherlands in Europe and Asia* (London and New York, 1968), p. 41; J. Black, *British*

Foreign Policy in the Age of Walpole (Edinburgh, 1985), p. 132; J. Aalbers, *De Republiek en de vrede van Europa* (Groningen, 1980), I, 47. I owe the last reference to the kindness of Dr Ph. M. Bosscher.

4. Quoted by Black, *British Foreign Policy*, p. 131.
5. H. Dunthorne, *The Maritime Powers 1721–1740: A Study of Anglo-Dutch Relations in the Age of Walpole* (New York and London, 1986), pp. 9, 42–6.
6. J. C. M. Warnsinck, *De Vloot van den Koning-Stadhouder, 1689–1690* (Amsterdam, 1934), pp. 15–16. The substance of the 1689 convention is recorded by E. B. Powley in *The Naval Side of King William's War* (London, 1972), pp. 368–9.
7. J. Ehrman, *The Navy in the War of William III, 1689–1697* (Cambridge, 1953), p. 251; Powley, *The Naval Side of King William's War*, p. 65.
8. A. N. Ryan, 'William III and the Brest Fleet in the Nine Years' War', in R. Hatton and J. S. Bromley, eds, *William III and Louis XIV: Essays 1680–1720 by and for Mark A. Thomson* (Liverpool, 1968), pp. 50–1.
9. G. van den Haute, *Les relations anglo-hollandaises au début du XVIIIe siècle* (Louvain, 1932), pp. 3, 76–9; Ehrman, *The Navy in the War of William III*, p. 310.
10. Dunthorne, *Maritime Powers*, p. 12.
11. G. Asaert *et al.*, eds, *Maritieme geschiedenis der Nederlanden*, 4 vols. (Bussum, 1974–8), III, p. 365.
12. Historical Manuscripts Commission [H.M.C.], *Finch Manuscripts* (71), II, p. 334.
13. S. B. Baxter, *William III* (London, 1966), p. 267; Warnsinck, *Vloot van den Koning-Stadhouder*, p. 127. P. Aubrey, *The Defeat of James Stuart's Armada, 1692* (Leicester, 1969), p. 52; Ehrman, *The Navy in the War of William III*, pp. 353–4; W. A. Aiken, ed., *The Conduct of the Earl of Nottingham* (New Haven, 1941), pp. 77–8.
14. Warnsinck, *De Vloot van den Koning-Stadhouder*, pp. ix, 133.
15. Aubrey, *The Defeat of James Stuart's Armada, 1692*, pp. 89, 128.
16. D. Coombs, *The Conduct of the Dutch: British Opinion and the Dutch Alliance during the War of the Spanish Succession* (The Hague, 1958), p. 7.
17. J. F. Bense, *Anglo-Dutch Relations from the Earliest Times to the Death of William the Third* (Oxford and The Hague, 1925), p. 132.
18. D. B. Horn, *Great Britain and Europe in the Eighteenth Century* (Oxford, 1967), p. 100; R. Hatton, *Diplomatic Relations between Great Britain and the Dutch Republic, 1714–1721* (London, 1950), p. 74.
19. Coombs, *Conduct of the Dutch*, p. 17.
20. H. Dunthorne, 'Prince and Republic: The House of Orange in Dutch and Anglo-Dutch Politics during the First Half of the Eighteenth Century', *Essays in European History in Honour of Ragnhild Hatton. Studies in History and Politics* IV (1985), p. 24; Dunthorne, *Maritime Powers*, p. 19.
21. Dunthorne, 'Prince and Republic', pp. 25–6; *Maritime Powers*, p. 243.
22. Horn, *Great Britain and Europe*, 87–90; A. C. Carter, *Neutrality or Commitment: The Evolution of Dutch Foreign Policy, 1667–1795*

(London, 1975), pp. 61, 69; P. Geyl, *Willem IV en Engeland tot 1748* (The Hague, 1924), p. 6; J. C. Boogman, 'Die holländische Tradition in der niederländischen Geschichte', in *Van spel en spelers* (The Hague, 1982): I owe this reference to the kindness of Dr Ph. M. Bosscher.

23. D. A. Miller, *Sir Joseph Yorke and Anglo-Dutch Relations, 1774-1780* (The Hague, 1970), pp. 118-19 gives a summary of the 1674 treaty.

24. R. Pares, *Colonial Blockade and Neutral Rights, 1739-1763* (Oxford, 1938), pp. 237-8. Dunthorne, *Maritime Powers*, p. 10.

25. Miller, *Sir Joseph Yorke*, pp. 116-17, gives the substance of the 1678 treaty.

26. Warnsinck, *De Vloot van den Koning-Stadhouder*, p. 55.

27. Van den Haute, *Les relations anglo-hollandaises*, pp. 315-17. J. S. Corbett, *England in the Mediterranean*, second edition (London, 1917), II, p. 498. Coombs, *Conduct of the Dutch*, pp. 52-3.

28. Coombs, *Conduct of the Dutch*, p. 38.

29. Van den Haute, *Les relations anglo-hollandaises*, p. 322.

30. J. B. Hattendorf, *England in the War of the Spanish Succession* (New York, 1987), p. 157.

31. Coombs, *Conduct of the Dutch*, p. 37; Hattendorf, *War of the Spanish Succession*, p. 156.

32. Coombs, *Conduct of the Dutch*, p. 80. Van den Haute, *Les relations anglo-hollandaises*, p. 323.

33. J. H. Owen, *War at Sea under Queen Anne, 1702-1708* (Cambridge, 1938), p. 103; J. R. Bruijn, *De Admiraliteit van Amsterdam in rustige jaren, 1713-1751* (Amsterdam and Haarlem, 1970), p. 9. H. W. Richmond, *The Navy in the War of 1739-48* (Cambridge, 1920), II, p. 169.

34. Hattendorf, *War of the Spanish Succession*, pp. 91-2.

35. J. S. Bromley, 'Some Zealand Privateering Instructions: Jacob Sautijn to Captain Salomon Reynders, 1707', in Hatton and Bromley, *William III and Louis XIV*, p. 163.

36. H. Wansinck, 'Holland and Six Allies: The Republic of the Seven United Provinces', in J. S. Bromley and E. H. Kossmann, eds, *Britain and the Netherlands IV* (The Hague, 1971), pp. 146-7; G. N. Clark, *The Dutch Alliance and the War against French Trade, 1688-1697* (Manchester, 1923), p. 52; Van den Haute, *Les relations anglo-hollandaises*, pp. 97, 299; J. Th. H. Verhees-Van Meer, *De Zeeuwse kaapvaart tijdens de Spaanse Successieoorlog 1702-1713* (Middelburg, 1986), pp. 73-118. I owe this last reference to the kindness of Professor J. R. Bruijn.

37. Warnsinck, *De Vloot van den Koning-Stadhouder*, pp. 6-7, 15-16.

38. For an exception see Owen, *War at Sea under Queen Anne*, p. 127.

39. Warnsinck, *De Vloot van den Koning-Stadhouder*, p. 79.

40. Public Record Office, London [P.R.O.]: SP 42/1 f. 31; H.M.C., *Finch Manuscripts*, III, p. 265; J. Burchett, *Memoirs of Transactions at Sea during the War with France ... 1688-1697* (London, 1703), p. 97.

41. Bruijn, *Admiraliteit van Amsterdam*, p. 33; P.R.O.: ADM 1/3242, Captain A. D. van der Gon to Admiralty, 20 April 1745 NS.

42. P.R.O.: SP 42/9 f. 164.
43. Horn, *Great Britain and Europe*, p. 92.
44. See his correspondence in P.R.O.: SP 84/237.
45. Quoted in Coombs, *Conduct of the Dutch*, pp. 280–1.
46. *Ibid.*, pp. 291, 321.
47. Quoted *Ibid.*, p. 292.
48. Hattendorf, *War of the Spanish Succession*, p. 159.
49. Dunthorne, *Maritime Powers*, p. 12.
50. Hatton, *Diplomatic Relations*, pp. 39–40, 74–80, 103, 121–5; Horn, *Great Britain and Europe*, p. 94; Bruijn, *Admiralteit van Amsterdam*, pp. 13–18.
51. D. B. Horn, *The British Diplomatic Service, 1689–1789* (Oxford, 1961), p. 18; see also n. 18 above.
52. Bruijn, *Admiraliteit van Amsterdam*, pp. 5, 91–8; Hatton, *Diplomatic Relations*, p. 16.
53. J. C. Boogman, 'Achtergronden, tendenties en tradities van het buitenlands beleid van Nederland (eind zestiende eeuw — 1940)', in *Van spel en spelers*, pp. 220–1. I owe this reference to Dr Ph. M. Bosscher.
54. Geyl, *Willem IV en Engeland*, p. 8; Boogman, 'Achtergronden, tendenties en tradities', p. 223.
55. Hatton, *Diplomatic Relations*, pp. 159, 217, in each case quoting Charles Whitworth.
56. Quoted in Black, *British Foreign Policy*, p. 123.
57. Quoted by Geyl, *Willem IV en Engeland*, p. 172.
58. Horn, *Great Britain and Europe*, p. 94; Hatton, *Diplomatic Relations*, p. 83; Coombs, *Conduct of the Dutch*, p. 176; Dunthorne, *Maritime Powers*, pp. 46–7.
59. Bruijn, *Admiraliteit van Amsterdam*, pp. 29, 165; J. Black, *Natural and Necessary Enemies: Anglo-French Relations in the Eighteenth Century* (London, 1986), p. 72.
60. Dunthorne, *Maritime Powers*, p. 181.
61. Black, *British Foreign Policy*, p. 96.
62. Richmond, *The Navy in the War of 1739–48*, II, p. 112; P.R.O.: SP 42/28 f. 4.
63. Bruijn, *Admiraliteit van Amsterdam*, pp. 33, 100, 128; P.R.O.: ADM 1/3242, Vice-Admiral C. Schrijver to Admiralty, 8 February 1745 NS.
64. P.R.O.: SP 42/28 ff. 46–8.
65. P.R.O.: ADM 1/3242, Vice-Admiral W. 't Hooft to Admiralty, 14 and 31 May 1745 NS; SP 42/29 ff. 77, 286, 442.
66. P.R.O.: ADM 1/3242, C. Schrijver to Admiralty, 24 December 1744 NS and 13 March 1745 NS; H. Grave to Admiralty 20 January 1745 NS; ADM 1/3243, W. 't Hooft to Admiralty, 12 June 1745 NS and 18 September 1745 NS. The 'kostpenningen' system is explained by Bruijn, *Admiraliteit van Amsterdam*, pp. 114–17.
67. P.R.O.: ADM 1/3243, W. 't Hooft to Admiralty, 9 November 1745 NS.
68. P.R.O.: Adm 1/3243, W. 't Hooft to Admiralty, 13 December 1745 NS; SP 42/29 ff. 442–4.

69. P.R.O.: SP 42/28 ff. 7, 20, 46–8, 109.
70. B. McL. Ranft, ed., *The Vernon Papers*, Navy Records Society, vol. 99 (London, 1958), p. 507.
71. Quoted by A. Kalshoven, *De diplomatieke verhouding tusschen Engeland en de Republiek der Vereen. Nederlanden 1747–1756* (The Hague, 1915), p. 23 n. 1.
72. Lord J. Russell (ed.), *Correspondence of John, Fourth Duke of Bedford* (London, 1842), I, p. 300; Bruijn, *Admiraliteit van Amsterdam*, p. 35.
73. Quoted by R. Lodge, *Studies in Eighteenth-Century Diplomacy, 1740–1748* (London, 1930), p. 175.
74. The best account of the skilful but unscrupulous manoeuvres of the British in Zeeland is in A. Porta, *Joan en Gerrit Corver: De politieke macht van Amsterdam, 1702–1748* (Assen, 1975), pp. 214–23.
75. Dunthorne, 'Prince and Republic' 128; Carter, *Neutrality or Commitment*, p. 69; S. B. Baxter, 'The Myth of the Grand Alliance in the Eighteenth Century', in P. R. Sellin and S. B. Baxter, *Anglo-Dutch Cross-Currents in the Seventeenth and Eighteenth Centuries* (Los Angeles, 1976), p. 54.
76. P.R.O.: SP 44/227 f. 182.
77. Russell, *Bedford Correspondence*, I, 266.
78. Horn, *Great Britain and Europe*, p. 100; Dunthorne, 'Prince and Republic', p. 30.
79. P.R.O.: ADM 1/3243, Schrijver to Admiralty, 11 January 1748 NS; SP 42/61, Admiralty to Lord Chesterfield, 1 January 1747 OS.
80. P.R.O.: ADM 1/3243, Schrijver to Admiralty, 23 January 1748 NS.
81. *Ibid.*, Schrijver to Admiralty, 19 January 1748 NS.
82. Bruijn, *Admiraliteit van Amsterdam*, p. 36.
83. P.R.O.: SP 42/61, Admiralty to Duke of Newcastle, 19 February 1747 OS.
84. Carter, *Neutrality or Commitment*, p. 73.
85. Geyl, *Willem IV en Engeland*, p. 144.
86. Pares, *Colonial Blockade and Neutral Rights*, pp. 231–5.
87. Geyl, *Willem IV en Engeland*, p. 291, n. 2.
88. Russell, *Bedford Correspondence*, I, 336.
89. R. E. J. Weber, *De seinboeken voor Nederlandse oorlogsvloten en konvooien tot 1690* (Amsterdam, 1982), pp. 3, 124–53.
90. For example, S. Martin-Leake, in G. Callender, ed., *The Life of Sir John Leake*, Navy Records Society, vols 52, 53 (London, 1920), I, pp. 247–8, 301, 305.
91. Bruijn, *Admiraliteit van Amsterdam*, pp. 9–12, 165; and 'Engelse scheepsbouwers op de Amsterdamse Admiraliteitswerf in de achttiende eeuw: enige aspecten', *Medelingen van de Nederlandse Vereniging voor Zeegeschiedenis* 25 (1972), pp. 18–20.
92. Horn, *The British Diplomatic Service*, p. 114.
93. F. Spencer, ed., *The Fourth Earl of Sandwich: Diplomatic Correspondence 1763–1765* (Manchester, 1961), p. 93.
94. Quoted in Aalbers, *De Republiek en de vrede van Europa*, p. 42.
95. P.R.O.: SP 44/228, f. 34.

96. Horn, *Great Britain and Europe*, pp. 101–103.
97. Pares, *Colonial Blockade and Neutral Rights*, p. 277.
98. A. Carter, 'How to revise Treaties without Negotiating: Commonsense, Mutual Fears and the Anglo-Dutch Trade Disputes of 1759', in R. Hatton and M. S. Anderson, eds, *Studies in Diplomatic History; Essays in Memory of David Bayne Horn* (London, 1970), pp. 214–15.
99. Carter, *Neutrality or Commitment*, pp. 88–9.
100. P.R.O.: SP 44/228, f. 54, 66.
101. Carter, *Neutrality or Commitment*, p. 73; P.R.O.: SP 42/29 f. 404; SP 44/228 f. 41; Carter, 'How to revise Treaties without Negotiation', p. 217.
102. Spencer, *Sandwich Diplomatic Correspondence*, p. 76.
103. *Ibid.*, pp. 83–4.
104. H. M. Scott, 'Sir Joseph Yorke, Dutch Politics and the Origins of the Fourth Anglo-Dutch War', *Historical Journal*, XXXI (1988), pp. 571–89; I am indebted to Dr Scott for allowing me to see this paper in advance of its publication.
105. Black, *Natural and Necessary Enemies*, p. 165; A. C. Carter, 'Britain as a European Power, from her Glorious Revolution to the French Revolutionary War', in Bromley and Kossmann, *Britain and the Netherlands in Europe and Asia*, p. 127.
106. Miller, *Sir Joseph Yorke*, p. 58.
107. *Ibid., passim*, especially pp. 41–50, 95.
108. E. S. van Eyck van Heslinga, 'De vlag dekt de lading: De Nederlandse koopvaardij in de Vierde Engelse Oorlog', *Tijdschrift voor Zeegeschiedenis* 1 (1982), p. 104.
109. Miller, *Sir Joseph Yorke*, pp. 77–87, 91–100. The most detailed account of the origins of this war is D. Syrett, *Neutral Rights and the War in the Narrow Seas, 1778–82* (Fort Leavenworth, Kansas, n.d.).
110. H.M.C. *Various Collections* (55) VI, 271. I owe this reference to Dr H. M. Scott.
111. Scott, 'Sir Joseph Yorke', *passim*.
112. J. Ehrman, *The Younger Pitt* (London, 1969ff.), II, pp. 520–43; A. Cobban, *Ambassadors and Secret Agents* (London, 1954), pp. 196–206.
113. Ehrman, *Younger Pitt*, II, p. 563; *Maritieme geschiedenis der Nederlanden*, III, p. 360; P.R.O.: HO 28/7 f. 235.
114. *Journal and Correspondence of William, Lord Auckland* (London, 1861–2), II, p. 382; I owe this reference to Dr R. B. Prud'homme van Reine.
115. Horn, *Great Britain and Europe*, p. 104; V. T. Harlow, *The Founding of the Second British Empire, 1763–1793*, 2 vols (London, 1952–64), I, pp. 130, 143–4; II, p. 365.

3

THE BRITISH AND NETHERLANDS ARMIES IN RELATION TO THE ANGLO-DUTCH ALLIANCE, 1688–1795

H. L. Zwitzer

The subtitle of the newsletter, '1688 Festivities', issued in the Netherlands and Britain in 1988, reads 'three hundred years of Anglo-Dutch friendship'. I am afraid, however, that historical evidence tells a different story, which compels us to qualify this statement. In my opinion it can be better viewed as an overstatement. For the sake of a successful celebration of the 'William and Mary' tercentenary, I do not see any harm in exaggerating just a little by laying emphasis on the friendship of the two countries. But we should not get carried away when we are talking about history, because this friendship seems to be more applicable to the last three or four decades than to the last three centuries.

Why England and the Dutch Republic, which were allies at the beginning of the Eighty Years' War against Spain, renewed their alliance in 1678 after three wars between 1652 and 1674 can, broadly speaking, be deduced from several phenomena. Among these were the aggressive policy of the French King Louis XIV, the anti-French House of Commons, the influential position of Stadholder William III with respect to the anti-French foreign policy of the Dutch Republic, and the marriage of William with his cousin Mary Stuart, daughter of King Charles II's brother, the Duke of York.

After the Peace of Westminster in 1674, by which the Third Dutch War was ended, Charles II pursued a neutral policy between the belligerents, Holland and his former ally France. France continued the war that started in 1672 and which nearly wiped out the United Provinces at the beginning.

The words 'neutral policy' have to be understood in the way Charles II interpreted them. A secret article of the Treaty of Westminster prescribed that Charles would not help the enemies of the Dutch. But this did not prevent him keeping English and Scottish troops in French service under command of the Duke of Monmouth, his illegitimate son. Even recruitment for this force was not hindered in Britain. And to extract subsidies from the French king, Charles II concluded one secret treaty after another with Louis XIV, promising to keep his anti-French parliament dissolved.[1] But England was not France, and Charles could not send his parliament home permanently. So on the reassembly of the chamber at the beginning of 1677, Charles had to enter into an alliance with the Dutch. For the French successes in the field made it quite probable that the coast of Flanders would remain in the hands of France, which was strategically a fatal threat to the British Isles, although it took nearly another year, because of the fickleness of the English king, before the Republic and England concluded a treaty in January 1678. They agreed to continue the war by joining their forces if France would not make peace. But a peace was signed at Nimwegen in August of that year. With the treaty of January 1678 the two countries entered into a sort of marriage of convenience. Another marriage of convenience, contracted two months earlier between Stadholder William III — half a Stuart through his mother — and his cousin Mary, was also one of the important stepping stones to the reluctant alliance between the Netherlands and England. Reluctant because the English did not trust the Dutch, nor did the latter the English. Moreover, public opinion in the Netherlands looked upon the royal court in England as a popish gathering. The Catholicism of Charles's successor, James II, Mary's father, was finally to bring William to England in November 1688. Three months later he and his wife became joint sovereigns of England, after both Houses of Parliament had declared it 'inconsistent with the safety and welfare of this Protestant kingdom to be governed by a popish prince'.[2] For our subject it is important to keep in mind that through William's policy England was now committed to help to preserve the freedom of Europe against Louis XIV's lust for power and his antagonistic feelings towards Protestantism. In fact this meant that both countries became involved in the war against France, which had already declared war against the Dutch in November 1688. This was followed by a Dutch declaration of war against France in March and an English one in May 1689. Earlier that year the Republic and England had signed a treaty, in which they agreed on a proportional strength of their fleets, although a similar treaty on the strength of their armies did not come off. This question seems to have been left to be worked out in practice.[3]

As a consequence, England's relations with France were reversed.

Charles II and James II had sought friendship with the Sun King, but, according to the Marquis of Halifax, William 'took England only in his way to France',[4] that is to say, in hostile relationship. For a country that considered the Dutch as their traditional enemies and trade rivals in general, this meant in fact a complete *volte face*. And although both countries remained allies until the Fourth Anglo-Dutch War in 1780, and after that until the Batavian Revolution in 1795, there was always a ring of that former antagonism and rivalry on both sides. It even showed up during the fight for decolonisation in Indonesia, during which years Britain played a dubious role, according to contemporary Dutch comments. It is also perceptible in the interpretation of historical events when the Dutch and English worked together. British military historiography in particular has a doubtful reputation in the Netherlands because of its one-sidedness. Notorious in this respect is the battle of Waterloo, for which English-speaking writers still use Captain Siborne's biased and incomplete story as a reliable source,[5] though the unreliability of his treatise was exposed in the nineteenth century by a Dutch Major, later Lieutenant-General W. J. Knoop.[6]

During King William's reign the Alliance stood under a single-headed leadership. He was commander during the campaigns in the War of the League of Augsburg, in the Netherlands known as the Nine Years' War, and the whole political and military strategy during this war was in his hands. After the peace of Ryswick, King William continued his policy of containment of Louis XIV, especially with the prospect of the legacy of the Hapsburg-Spanish king, Charles II, whose death had been anticipated throughout Europe from the moment he came to the throne in 1665. Eventually he died in 1700, thirty-five years later. In his testament this mentally weak prince laid down that the whole Spanish realm would be left to Philip V of Anjou, grandson of Louis XIV. The States-General and the King-Stadholder accepted the testament as a *fait accompli* and recognised Philip of Anjou as King of Spain and of her colonies all over the world. This frustrated the partition treaties, concluded after the Peace of Ryswick between William and the French king, dividing the realm between Bourbon and Hapsburg claimants. The emperor, however, kept the right of inheritance for his Hapsburg family and opened hostilities against the Spanish possessions in Italy. Perhaps that would have ended the matter, if the French king had not occupied the Spanish Southern Netherlands (modern Belgium) ordering the governor there to obey all instructions given from Paris. But this was not enough. In the first half of 1701, Louis XIV designated Philip

of Anjou as his only successor to the throne of France. This might lead
to an intolerable domination by France of Europe and the rest of the
world. The English Parliament, which had thus far seen King William's
efforts concerning the Spanish inheritance as superfluous, now began
to understand the goals of this policy to keep expansionist France under
control in order to restore the balance of power in Europe. Perhaps
drunk with his success, Louis XIV deeply insulted the English later in
the year by recognising James Edward as king of England and Scotland.
James Edward was a son of the refugee James II, who died in France in
September 1701. Quite inconsistent with the terms of the Peace of
Ryswick, this move of the French king had the effect of increasing
English support for William's policy of taming the aspirations of
Louis XIV. From the summer of 1701, war seemed inevitable and, in
consideration of his deteriorating health, William chose John Churchill,
Earl of Marlborough, as the man to carry out his policy. Before he died
in March 1702 he appointed him extraordinary ambassador to the
Dutch Republic and Commander-in-Chief of the English forces that
had been sent to Holland. Marlborough, in his former capacity, and the
Grand Pensionary of Holland, Anthonie Heinsius, prepared the Grand
Alliance of the Hague between England, the Republic and the Emperor,
which declared war on France simultaneously on 15 May 1702. I shall
not dwell on the Emperor Leopold, but leave him in Vienna and confine
myself to the ins and outs and the further development of the alliance
between the Netherlands and England and to the co-operation of their
troops in the field. The traditional and natural enemies, Holland and
England, were now staunch allies for the period of the conflict, as they
were not to be again until Napoleon's Hundred Days and the Second
World War. In particular I shall examine the position of the Captain-
General, John Churchill (from 1702 Duke of Marlborough), in relation
to the contribution that Holland and England made to their forces on
the Continent, and some other topics concerning the alliance during the
rest of the eighteenth century.

Until now it has been generally understood among historians that
Marlborough was appointed Captain-General of both the English and
the Dutch armies. This, however, is a simplification of his real position,
which was stated in a secret decree of the States-General of 30 June
1702, agreed to by Marlborough three days later. The first article of the
decree said that Dutch troops could be joined with the army commanded
by the Captain-General of Her Majesty, Queen Anne. English troops
also could be joined with the army commanded by the General of the

Republic. Other articles said that the Captain-General of the English troops and the General commanding the troops of the Republic would consult each other on all matters concerning operations in the field. Further, that the Captain-General would always act in accordance with the Field Deputies, the representatives of the States-General in the Dutch army and the General of the army of the States. Special instructions for the Dutch General in command said it was his duty to maintain good relations with Marlborough, but to avoid everything that would be contrary to the interests of the Dutch army, or harmful to the honour and dignity of the Republic.[7] It is therefore quite clear that Marlborough's position was not exactly that of a Commander-in-Chief with all the other generals subordinate to him, which indeed would have been against the honour and dignity of the Republic. But there were other and less abstract arguments. The Dutch army was more than twice as big as the English army on the Continent: 100,000 against 40,000; later in the war the Dutch troops provisionally amounted to 130,000 men and the English to 70,000. These figures need some explanation. At the beginning of the war the standing army of the States-General had a strength of some 45,000 men. In the course of the war this was raised to 75,000. In addition to this, 42,000 men were hired from German principalities, plus 15,000 men who were not paid out of the ordinary and extraordinary budgets, but from contributions raised in the occupied parts of the Southern Netherlands. As for the English troops, I mentioned already that these were increased during the course of the war to 70,000; 20,000 men of British nationality, the remainder having been mainly recruited in Germany. What made the situation more complicated is that part of the troops were half in the pay of England and half in the pay of the Dutch Republic. So, of the 132,000 men on the Dutch and 70,000 men on the English side, 56,000 were for the joint account of England and the Republic. This, however, does not alter the fact that the Dutch were responsible for the greater part both of the expense and the numbers of the land forces. Therefore it is hardly surprising that the States-General were reluctant to give Marlborough full power over their army, objectively one of the best they had ever brought on to the field. Another reason for the highly restrictive provisions in which Marlborough's authority became embedded was that the States-General did not want to run the risk that Dutch political and military goals might be neglected and made subordinate to British interests. The Field Deputies have sometimes been seen by British and also by some Dutch historians as meddlers, crossing Marlborough's

plans. But their position was in fact quite a natural one, while for the
Dutch the very existence of their country was at stake. One unsuccessful
allied military enterprise could have been much more dangerous for the
safety of the Dutch territory than for the British Isles, surrounded as
they were by the Channel and the high seas, and therefore in a much
safer strategic position.

The first years of the war, up to 1705, are characterised by many
disputes and differences of opinion between Marlborough and the
Dutch generals. After the sieges and the capture of Liège in 1702 and
Bonn in 1703 for example, the Dutch generals fell into a rage because
Marlborough refused to let them sign the capitulation document.
Complaining to the States-General about this unwarranted extension of
Marlborough's authority, the Dutch generals insisted that the troops of
the Republic had greatly exceeded the numbers of the English, and that
during the siege of Bonn only Dutch troops in Dutch pay had been
active. General Van Reede van Ginkel, Earl of Athlone, one of the
Dutch generals who fought in 1690 and afterwards against the French
in Ireland, wrote to the States-General that King William had never had
such pretensions, while General Obdam told the States-General that, if
things went on like this, everything would come under command of a
foreign general, and that Mylord Marlborough would become Captain-
General of the Republic's troops as well as the English.[8] This latter
statement clearly indicates that in the United Provinces Marlborough
was not considered to be the one and only Commander-in-Chief. The
continual quarrels between Marlborough and one of the most competent
Dutch generals, Frederik Johan van Baer van Slangenburg, give a
characteristic picture of how they felt about the position of the British
general. Slangenburg was a Catholic nobleman from the Province of
Guelders. His military capacities seemed not inferior to those of
Marlborough, but his fits of rage and anger in public made him inferior
to Marlborough as a diplomat. Slangenburg's reports and letters are
instructive, especially because they are a sort of antidote against the
usually somewhat hagiographic literature on Marlborough. His reports
about the attempt on the Dyle position in August 1705 — a plan
designed by Marlborough without consulting the Dutch generals, except
Field Marshal Auerquerque — and the advance towards the French
positions behind the river Yssche, some 12 kilometres from Brussels,
tell us that after they reached the French line, the whole allied army
remained idle for the rest of the day. One reason was that General
Charles Churchill, Marlborough's brother, whose task it was to outflank

the French by a concealed march with his corps through the Forest of Soignies, lost his way in the wood and was therefore not able to threaten the French rear — Marlborough's essentially modern tactical manoeuvre. In fact the general returned empty-handed and his corps was now going to be placed opposite the French right wing. Another reason was that the artillery was placed behind the baggage train, a situation causing great delay. By the time Charles Churchill had completed his manoeuvre, it was between 5 and 6 o'clock in the afternoon. The commander of the Dutch troops, Field Marshal Auerquerque, had been ready to mount the attack since 10 o'clock in the morning, but had not received any advice or plan of attack. At the request of the Dutch Field Deputies, a council of war was held in the open air at the end of the afternoon. During this consultation Marlborough and Slangenburg got into a violent argument, the latter saying that he would obey any order, but that he did not want to take any responsibility for a plan of which he had not had any knowledge in advance. Slangenburg even claimed that in fact an attack had not been intended at all, and that a pretext was being sought to blame the Dutch generals for the failure of the plan. Slangenburg's arguments for his accusation were that, although Charles Churchill's corps had come back during the council of war, no order to charge had been issued yet; and further, that no artillery had been mounted yet, and that the four commanders who would have had to lead the crossings over the river Yssche were still not designated. In short, all preparations had failed.[9] I shall not dwell too long on this incident, but it is significant that the commander of the French troops opposite Marlborough, Marshal Villeroy, wrote in his report to the king: 'Il ne faut pas douter que le Duc de Marlborough jettera la faute sur M.M. les Etats',[10] which was exactly what happened when Marlborough wrote his bulletin, intended for publication in England, in which he said: 'The Deputies of the States, having consulted with their other generals, would not give their consent, so that the proposed attack was countermanded'.[11] This rendering of events was repeated in letters which Marlborough wrote to foreign heads of state and to ministers. There had been more of these incidents; two years earlier, in 1703, at Ekeren, a little north of Antwerp, Marlborough, leading an army farther to the east near Huy, had refused to send reinforcements for the attack on Antwerp,[12] much to the annoyance of Slangenburg. In 1705, about a month before the incident at the Yssche crossing, Marlborough failed to take Louvain, in spite of Slangenburg urging him to take his chance.[13] This time too Marshal

Villeroy is our witness; he wrote to the French king: 'si le Duc de Marlborough avait marché tout de suite, il serait arrivé à Louvain avant nous'.[14]

However, Slangenburg's criticism of Marlborough was not in the interest of the Republic. The States-General wanted to avoid a rupture with Marlborough or with the English government at all costs. The result was that the Catholic Slangenburg, not very popular with the Dutch public, in contrast to the Protestant Marlborough, was sacrificed in the interest of the alliance. Half a decade later, the States-General again rejected all French offers to bring about a separate peace, likewise for the sake of the alliance, and, of course, of the Republic. A British Tory government, however, which had replaced the former Whigs, thought that a peace policy would be much more advantageous to Britain. This led to secret British negotiations with France without consulting the Dutch allies, who were completely outsmarted by the British. The outcome was that the Duke of Marlborough, the English champion of the alliance, was discharged from service. The Anglo-Dutch Treaty, concluded in 1709, which guaranteed the Republic a barrier of fortresses in the Southern Netherlands opposite the French border, was violated. A peace treaty was agreed in 1713, which was very profitable to the British and to the French, but not to the United Provinces, which were fobbed off with a mere pittance. Considering this, it is peculiar to read in an English book that the favourable peace terms for Britain 'reflected her disproportionate contribution to the war effort, in men, ships and money'.[15] I am afraid that this statement is rather contrary to the facts, and I shall go into it more deeply. Confining myself to the war efforts on land, I should like to recollect that during the three former Dutch wars against England in the seventeenth century, and the wars against France since 1672, by the year of the Peace of Utrecht the public debt of the Republic had increased to 240 million guilders. Of this sum, 174 millions had been negotiated during the War of the Spanish Succession.[16] With a population of 1.9 million people in the Republic, this means a per capita debt of 91 guilders, simply and solely for the negotiated loans during the War of the Spanish Succession. Total expenditure on war costs for the Republic during the years 1702 to 1713 amounted to 348.5 million guilders;[17] a per capita expenditure of 183 guilders. Converting pounds to guilders, the British figures for the same period are: negotiated loans, 308.7 million guilders; government expenditure, 982.8 million guilders.[18] With a population of about 9.3 million in the British Isles, this means a per capita debt of 33 guilders for loans and a total expenditure of 106 guilders per capita. Compared with the figures of the Republic, the British debt per head of the population was 58 guilders less than in the United Provinces. The war expenditure was 77 guilders less per head of the population. According to the absolute figures, the British contribution does indeed seem disproportionate, but comparatively speaking the Dutch were far worse off. Moreover, the Dutch figures concern only the army; the British refer to both army and navy.

The War of the Spanish Succession heralded the decline of the Dutch Republic as a great power. In former years she had been able to play this role because then she had been able to bear the financial burden of large armies and/or fleets. After 1713 she lost this ability, which had enormously supported her 'prestige' and 'credit' among the nations in Europe. Strangely enough, she did not immediately disappear from the European political scene as an influential power. Traditionally most people continued to see the Republic as the nation which had taken the lead against the policy of Louis XIV. In this respect one might speak of a sort of time gap with respect to the estimation of the real value of the actual Dutch position in the European scene. Despite England's not very faithful behaviour towards her ally at the end of the War of the Spanish Succession — characterised by Sir Winston Churchill as 'black treachery' — both countries, Britain and the United Provinces, maintained their alliance: Britain, because of the standing Dutch army, which she expected, could be used as a sort of 'force in being' on the Continent. Because an unbalanced Europe would also endanger Britain herself and could lay her open to an invasion, this army could be strengthened with a newly raised expeditionary force from Britain, at any moment when a country in Europe endangered the balance of power. According to the treaties between the two countries, in which the Dutch had guaranteed the Protestant succession in Britain, the Dutch troops could be used in Britain against Jacobite revolts. Four times in the eighteenth century the Dutch army fulfilled this obligation by sending a force of 6,000 men each time the Catholic Stuart Pretender invaded Scotland, namely in 1715, 1719, 1744 and 1745.

As for the Republic, she remained loyal to the alliance for the greater part of the century. Financially exhausted after the War of the Spanish Succession, the United Provinces had lost their ability to take the lead in maintaining the balance of power on the Continent. For this purpose, which was important for an undisturbed development of Dutch trade, the Republic had waged war against Louis XIV for forty years. Now that the Peace of Utrecht had restored the balance of power, the safest thing for the Republic was to hold on to the new status quo. As we have seen, however, this did not mean that the Republic remained fully neutral, like modern Switzerland. The alliance with England was lived up to and the barrier of fortified towns (much reduced by the new treaty) emphasised her commitment to European affairs. This also kept the Republic tied to Austria which, as a result of the Peace of Utrecht, had assumed power in the Southern Netherlands from Spain. Good relations with Austria were important to the Republic. However, in 1731 the Republic had to pay a price in the shape of compulsory guarantees, together with Britain, of the Pragmatic Sanction that regulated the succession to the Hapsburg possessions. This guarantee, later acceded to by other countries, also served as an instrument to maintain the status quo on the Continent. However, several nations which had signed the Pragmatic Sanction, for instance, France and Prussia, did not want to recognise Maria Theresia as the lawful successor of her father, Charles VI, after his death in October 1740. This meant that now the Austrian-Hapsburg possessions were at stake, just as the Spanish had been forty years before.

Because the Republic was ill-prepared for a war, it now tried to remain neutral *vis-à-vis* France, but at the same time to fulfil its obligations towards Austria, in helping her with subsidies, and later with troops. A peculiar feature of the War of the Austrian Succession was, that of the two allies, Holland and Britain, only the latter officially declared war on France. Formally, the Republic remained neutral and tried to start negotiations between France and Great Britain, where a more war-minded government saw the conflict as an opportunity to enlarge her colonial possessions. The British government played a waiting game and thwarted Dutch mediation. The result was that France, in the course of 1744, still without declaring war on the Republic, opened hostilities against the barrier towns in the Southern Netherlands. This happened at the moment when the Dutch sent 6,000 men from the barrier garrisons to Britain to help to oust one of the Pretender's movements. The barrier towns, now with a much reduced complement of troops, fell to the French one after another. This aroused mere mockery in England. In the Republic, however, the scapegoat was the English General Wade, commander of the British expeditionary force in the Southern Netherlands, who had refused to send his troops into the barrier towns to strengthen the weakened garrisons. This kind of trouble, these mutual accusations of incompetence, are typical symptoms of the co-operation of the Dutch and English armies.

The difference with the War of the Spanish Succession is the position of the Republic compared to that of England. At the beginning of the conflict over the Spanish succession, both countries were more or less evenly matched. Now, forty years later, the Republic was no longer well-matched to Britain. The British representative at the Hague, Robert Hampden Trevor, very well understood the weak position of the Republic and tried to do as much as possible to help her and to tone down the claims of the warlike party in the British government. The champions of the war, however, gained greater power in the government in 1745, which a year later led to the replacement of Trevor by John Montagu, Earl of Sandwich, who had eyes only for the interests of Britain. The Republic now became fully dragged into the fighting, firstly, by the British attitude, and secondly, by the French decision to open hostilities in the Southern Netherlands. There the quarrelling British, Dutch and Austrian generals were replaced by one Commander-in-Chief of the allied armies, the Duke of Cumberland, son of King George II. He was no Marlborough however, and the first campaign under his command, in 1745, started with the defeat at Fontenoy. In the same year he disappeared with his whole army to Britain where he had to face a new invasion of the Pretender in Scotland. Returning to the Continent in 1746 he could not prevent the French from conquering the greater part of the Southern Netherlands under the very able Maréchal de Saxe, who even invaded the territory of the Republic in 1747, occupying several significant Dutch towns.[19]

A very important consequence of the successes of the French army was that in the Republic the oligarchical government was accused of incompetence, and the demands for William IV, the Frisian Nassau, became louder and louder. His father had been heir to the childless King William III, and had inherited the title 'Prince of Orange'. Up to that moment William IV had been kept from the function of stadholder in four of the seven provinces. Although at first sight an internal Dutch affair, the whole question had virtually everything to do with the Dutch–British Alliance. William IV's wife, Princess Anne of Hanover, was a daughter of George II. I shall not dwell on the king's motives for giving his daughter in marriage to a not so handsome and not so very influential prince on the Continent. All I want to say about it is that William's title, 'Prince of Orange', inspired respect, and the fact that the

British king was also Elector of Hanover had something to do with it. The king hoped to gain in prestige with this marriage. In Britain the name 'Orange' was linked with the 'Glorious Revolution', but the name 'Hanover', did not make any impression at all. George II had high hopes of the marriage and expected the Republic to install his son-in-law in due course as stadholder in each of the seven provinces, although British governments remained quite discreet towards the governing anti-Orange oligarchy on this point. During the Austrian War of Succession however, the British worked more openly in favour of the Frisian stadholder and the pro-Orange party in the Republic. This link between Orange and Britain continued during the rest of the eighteenth century. The Orange party functioned as a guarantee to Britain that the alliance would not be jeopardised. At the same time however, being now convinced of the weakness of the Republic, she was looking for a stronger ally on the Continent. Therefore it seems no coincidence that Britain, Prussia and the Republic concluded a Triple Alliance in 1788, balancing the French–Austrian connection, which had existed since the Seven Years' War. In this treaty too the stadholdership was guaranteed by Britain and Prussia.

The French Revolution toppled everything and made France the enemy of the *Ancien Régime* states in Europe, including Austria. As fifty years before, Austria now became the ally of Britain and of the Republic. During the War of the First Coalition, which began in 1793 after France had declared war on Britain, the Republic, Austria and Prussia, the British and Dutch armies fought together against a common enemy for the last time in the eighteenth century. This co-operation, however, was not much of a success. There was no uniformity in command. The Duke of York, commander of the British Expeditionary Force of 27,000 men (15,000 British and 12,000 Hanoverians and Hessians) did not want to serve under the eldest son of Stadholder Prince William V, the acting commander of the Dutch troops. William, conversely, did not want to do the opposite. So both armies acted nearly independently with only minimal co-operation. The Duke of York, son of King George III, had been ordered by the British government to spare his troops as much as possible. Putting them under an overall Dutch command might frustrate this order. Prince William was afraid that the Dutch army, coming under York's command, would be kept too long in the Austrian or Southern Netherlands. Fighting the French there would lead to losses of men, horses and material, and this would increase the risk that too few troops would be left to defend the territory of the

Republic. The rather low standard of the expeditionary force may have been another argument. Henry Calvert, one of York's staff-officers, wrote in his journal about the British troops: 'They much resembled Falstaff's men and were as lightly clad as any carmagnole battalion',[20] and a Dutch source says that some battalions had more women than men.[21] Foreign and Dutch commentators are unanimous about the bad discipline in York's army. A report from Vienna speaks about 'la détestable conduite des soldats du Duc d'York, qui sous un chef toujours plongé dans l'ivresse, ont commis partout des violences affreuses'.[22] The Dutch Grand Pensionary, Van de Spiegel, wrote: 'Even the most reasonable people do not hesitate to declare openly that, although it is degrading to humiliate oneself before a victorious enemy, it is much more degrading to see in our country a foreign army over which we have no say, and which permits itself no fewer disorders than the enemy would have committed'.[23] York attributed the bad discipline (which had not prevented good fighting now and then) to the billeting of his troops in a foreign country, with people expressing themselves in a language which was utterly unintelligible to the English officers and men.[24] This also played a role when the British troops began to leave the Republic in January 1795, after the French had conquered the southern and western parts of the country. The fact was that in the English marching orders many, if not most Dutch topographical names had been corrupted, which was one of the reasons why these troops lost their way during their retreat to Germany.[25] Another reason was the unprecedentedly atrocious weather. A German officer serving in the British force, and who later, in 1812, served in Napoleon's army during the campaign in Russia, wrote in his memoirs that the march through the centre of the Dutch Republic to the German border in 1795 was much more disastrous than the retreat through the Russian plains.[26]

After their defeat by the French general, Pichegru, who led his army over the frozen rivers which formed the natural Dutch defence line, the United Provinces became the Batavian Republic, and consequently an ally of France and an enemy of Britain. Except for the Fourth Anglo-Dutch War, the alliance had lasted more than a century.

At first sight it is rather surprising that the co-operation of the British and Dutch armies had no traceable impact on the organisational or tactical structure of their land forces during the period of the alliance. Probably the effects of the military revolution that began in the sixteenth century had, by 1650, created the same sort of military doctrine throughout Europe. Constitutional differences between the two countries, a monarchy and a confederation respectively, may have had influence on the organisational structure of both armies. These differences needed different bureaucracies to handle a complicated body like an army. A good example is the system of payment which, because of its constitutional structure, was much more complicated and decentralised in the Republic than in Britain.

Though they were equals at the start of the alliance, by the end of the War of the Spanish Succession Britain outmatched the Republic. This development was largely the result of the policy of resistance to French expansionism begun by Stadholder William III, and continued by him as king of England. It was difficult to understand for a generation of Dutch politicians who had grown up in a time when nothing could be arranged on the Continent without the foreknowledge of the United Provinces. Just as in 1945 the majority of politicians in the Netherlands could not come to terms with the idea that the Dutch colonial realm had come to an end, the politicians in 1713 and afterwards were out of date in appreciating the declining position of the Republic. They were unable to give up the hope that the Republic, which had fought off France, England, Münster and Cologne in 1672, might once more halt her decline, and rise from the ashes like a phoenix. Her demographical, territorial and financial situation however, did not permit the Republic to become a 'Phoenix Too Frequent'. In plain English she had become a minor power, although tradition denied her this role until about 1750, after which her influence in European affairs agreed more with her position as a small country among greater states like Britain, France, Austria and Prussia. Neutrality, not commitment, became the Republic's policy after 1750, but the idea that a careful alliance could be favourable to her remained alive throughout the eighteenth century. This idea, and the connection of the House of Orange with England, explains why its alliance continued, although the Republic at the same time aimed at neutrality.

The policy of the Kingdom of the Netherlands in the nineteenth and twentieth century appears less open and based on a naïve sort of Macchiavellianism, this same being in two minds. Her neutral policy was now built on the supposition that an invisible alliance with Britain would guarantee the independence of the Netherlands. I am afraid that this kind of unworldly ingenuousness might also have inspired the organisers of the 1688 celebration to lay emphasis on the term *friendship*, while after all, *raison d'état* was always the leading principle in both countries.

NOTES

1. M. Ashley, *England in the Seventeenth Century* (Harmondsworth, 1965), p. 138 ff; M. A. M. Franken, *Coenraad van Beuningen's politieke en diplomatieke aktiviteiten in de jaren 1667-1684* (Groningen, 1966), p. 129.
2. Ashley, *England*, p. 179.
3. F. J. G. ten Raa, F. de Bas, J. W. Wijn, *Het Staatsche leger*, 8 vols (Breda, The Hague, 1913-64), VIII, book 1, p. 18.
4. Ashley, *England*, p. 180.
5. W. Siborne, *History of the War in France and Belgium in 1815* (London, 1844).
6. W. J. Knoop, *Beschouwingen over Siborne's geschiedenis van den oorlog van 1815 in Frankrijk en de Nederlanden en wederlegging van de, in dat werk voorkomende, beschuldigingen tegen het Nederlandsche leger* (Breda, 1846); see also: F. de Bas and J. de T'Serclaes de Wommersom, *La Campagne de 1815 au Pays-Bas*, 3 vols (Brussels, 1908-09). A modern Dutch book on Waterloo is: A. Vels Heyn, *Glorie zonder helden* (Amsterdam, 1974). This is a critical study in which British self-display and blown-up Dutch nationalism are avoided.
7. Ten Raa, De Bas, Wijn, *Staatsche leger*, VIII, book 1, pp. 110-12, 696-8.
8. *Ibid.*, p. 250.
9. *Ibid.*, pp. 619-27.
10. *Ibid.*, p. 627.
11. *Ibid.*, p. 628; see also Marlborough's letter to the States-General on p. 627.
12. *Ibid.*, p. 278 ff.
13. *Ibid.*, p. 598.
14. *Ibid.*, p. 597.
15. G. Parker, 'The Emergence of Modern Finance in Europe 1500-1700', in C. M. Cipolla, ed., *The Fontana Economic History of Europe II. The Sixteenth and Seventeenth Centuries* (Glasgow, 1974), pp. 527-594.
16. J. Aalbers, 'Holland's Financial Problems (1713-1733) and the Wars against Louis XIV', in A. C. Duke and C. A. Tamse, eds, *Britain and the Netherlands. Papers delivered to the Sixth Anglo-Dutch Historical Conference* (The Hague, 1977), pp. 81-2; Algemeen Rijksarchief, The Hague: Archief Staten-Generaal, Staten van Oorlog after 1713, Chapter: 'Staat van alle de capitaalen genegotieert ten comptoire van de Unie'. From this source I extracted in round figures negotiated sums for war purposes between 1702 and 1713, totalling 31 million guilders, not mentioned by Aalbers.
17. Ten Raa, De Bas, Wijn, *Staatsche leger*, VII, p. 463; VIII, book 1, pp. 393-414.
18. Parker, 'Emergence', p. 580. For the rate of exchange see N. W. Posthumus, *Nederlandsche prijsgeschiedenis*, 2 vols (Leiden, 1943-64), I, pp. 594-625.
19. For the position of the United Provinces during the War of the Austrian Succession see P. Geyl, *Willem IV en England tot 1748 (Vrede van Aken)* (The Hague, 1924), *passim*.

20. F. H. A. Sabron, *De oorlog van 1794–1795 op het grondgebied van de Republiek der Vereenigde Nederlanden*, 2 vols (Breda, 1891–3), I, p. 40.
21. *Ibid.*, I, p. 41.
22. *Ibid.*, I, p. 218.
23. *Ibid.*, II, p. 10.
24. *Ibid.*, I, p. 219.
25. *Ibid.*, II, p. 223.
26. *Ibid.*, II, p. 225, footnote 1.

4

'A VERY UNPLEASANT RELATIONSHIP'. TRADE AND STRATEGY IN THE EASTERN SEAS: ANGLO-DUTCH RELATIONS IN THE NINETEENTH CENTURY FROM A COLONIAL PERSPECTIVE

J. A. de Moor

The year was 1800, the date the 4th of September. Two Spanish merchant vessels — the *Paz* and the *Esmeralda*, loaded with food, arms, ammunition and other military equipment — were anchored in the Mediterranean, in the roads of Barcelona. The crew, consisting of Spanish and Dutch seamen and Dutch military officers, were already aboard. Both ships had been chartered by the Dutch ambassador in Madrid, Johan Valckenaar. The next day, 5 September, 300 Spanish troops were to embark, with destination Batavia, in Java. The Spanish king, Charles IV, had himself put these troops at Valckenaar's disposal. They were 300 of the best Swiss soldiers from the garrison at Mallorca. This was 'to demonstrate our friendship with the Batavian Republic and simultaneously to protect the settlements of the Republic in Java and surroundings against an expected attack by our common enemy', in accordance with the treaty which Valckenaar had lately concluded with the king.[1] It was Valckenaar's finest hour. The expedition, insignificant as it may seem to us, set the seal on many months of work. A shrewd diplomat, a confirmed left-wing Dutch patriot, and a workaholic, he had worked frantically to achieve this success — a combined Dutch–Spanish military expedition to save the riches of Java from capture by the greedy British.

But then, on that selfsame 4th of September, at 9.30 in the evening, a Swedish trading vessel, *Die Hoffnung*, suddenly loomed up from the dark. Almost unnoticed, silently and swiftly gliding across the water, it approached the two ships. Quick as lightning the ships were boarded by scores of English seamen and soldiers. There was hardly any resistance. A Dutch seaman was killed; others, including military officers, were taken prisoner. Sails were hoisted, and within a quarter of an hour the *Paz* and *Esmeralda* disappeared in the night. From the fortifications on shore not a single gunshot was fired. Thus Valckenaar's exertions of years were all undone.

The news shattered him. Only much later was he able to reconstruct what had happened. The English, knowing that an expedition to Java was about to set sail, decided to capture the ships taking part in it. Two British warships boarded a neutral Swedish merchant vessel in the Mediterranean and forced the captain at gunpoint to take English seamen and soldiers on board, hide them and carry them unseen to the Spanish ships. 'A mean and shameful thing to do', Valckenaar exclaimed furiously, 'an ignoble abuse of a neutral flag!'[2] Since 1795, the Government of the Batavian Republic, one of France's most obedient allies, had lived in constant worry over the fate of the Dutch colonial possessions spread all over the globe. The British had begun to conquer these in order to prevent a French *coup d'état.* Two areas were of special importance — Surinam and Java. They had to be retained at all costs. 'Think of the immense treasures of those settlements', Valckenaar wrote from Madrid, 'if Britain gains control over them, it will be able to keep up the fighting for years'.[3] There was, of course, some truth in Valckenaar's statement, especially with regard to Surinam, which had developed into a rich plantation colony in the eighteenth century. Its shipments of coffee, sugar, cocoa and other commercial crops had become increasingly important for the Dutch economy, and even surpassed the Dutch East India Company trade in value. So Valckenaar was right in fixing attention upon Surinam first, when he became Dutch ambassador to the Spanish king in 1797. Initially, he wanted to recruit no fewer than 6,000 men in Spain for service in the Dutch colonies. It was in Madrid at the Spanish court that he exerted all his talents, strength and money to persuade, convince and bribe the authorities to assist him with men and arms. During his first stay in Spain he managed with superhuman effort to obtain a mere 650 Swiss soldiers in Spanish service for Surinam. They departed from Cadiz in 1798. All the preparations were carried out secretly, not just because of the English, but more especially because the contract between the Spanish king and the Swiss companies explicitly forbade the use of the troops overseas! That they were being sent to Surinam was kept a secret even from the soldiers until the eve of their departure. When the Swiss, under the command of the Spanish nobleman, Don Manuel D'Amparán, finally arrived in Surinam in 1799, in a very bad mood, I suppose, they caused strong feelings of resentment, since they were much better paid than the soldiers already present in the colony.

Governor Friderici felt obliged to pay all the forces equally, and thus raised the pay of the others, much to the annoyance of the planters, who were to be saddled with the extra costs. And to pay for the colony's defence was the last thing they wanted to do! Finally, in August 1799, barely a few months after the arrival of the Swiss, the long-expected British fleet under Hugh Seymour appeared. There were no Dutch naval forces present in Surinam, since the naval squadron led by Admiral Van Raders had been annihilated at the battle of Camperdown in 1797. Despite the arrival of the Swiss, Governor Friderici decided, under heavy pressure from the planters, not to defend the colony, but to surrender at once. Sheer relief was felt throughout Surinam: 'Luckily no property is damaged'. According to the planters this was the best thing for the colony's economy. Part of the surrendered goods were the Swiss. Most of them, 350, passed into British service; the remainder were transported to Spain by British ships in the winter of 1799 and were cast ashore somewhere on a beach without food, shoes or proper clothes, most of them ill.[4] Valckenaar received the message of Surinam's surrender at the end of 1799, while he was just starting his campaign for a relief expedition to Java. The best thing he could do was to cover up the bad news and keep it from the king. Now that Surinam was lost, Java was all the more important. With characteristic boldness he told the king: 'You promised me 1,200 Swiss; 600 of them went to Surinam, so I claim another 600 for Java'.[5] The king, obviously unaware of the outcome of the Surinam expedition, reacted rather angrily: 'What do you mean, another 600! Where are my 600 Swiss guards who went to Surinam? We haven't received any message from them'.[6] Yet Valckenaar succeeded in his efforts by dint of his magnificent powers of persuasion, and of course his money. On 31 May 1800, a treaty was signed, providing for 300 Swiss guards from the Courten regiment on Mallorca. It even provided for a Catholic priest to accompany the forces, and stipulated that in case of his premature death, a new priest should be sent in order not to leave the forces deprived of spiritual care. Even in Spain, Batavia's reputation as the graveyard of the East must have been known!

All this, Valckenaar's work of many years, was undone in less than a quarter of an hour on that quiet September evening. He wrote home: 'A terrible loss which has struck me profoundly since all my work has been swept away in a few moments, and also a new and terrible loss for our country'.[7] Two Dutch medical officers, who were to accompany the troops and had witnessed the surprise attack from the beach, commented: 'It was all due to the dreadful carelessness and damned sleepiness of the Spanish authorities'. And, they added, in case of a future expedition, the organisation should not be left to the Spaniards, for 'they are miserable and worthless and their rulers are the craziest of all!'[8]

Valckenaar's efforts to build up and reconstruct the colonial defence were hardly senseless, but they came too late. From 1800 onwards British naval squadrons launched surprise attacks on Java and other islands in the Archipelago. Commodore Ball blockaded Batavia harbour and bombarded the island of Onrust. In fact, he could easily have captured Batavia — the city was hardly defended — had it not been for his own shortage of provisions and ammunition. In the next few years, British naval pressure upon the Dutch settlements was constantly increased, until in 1806 Britain dealt a decisive blow by destroying 26 merchant vessels in the roadstead of Batavia under Admiral Pellew.

This book is concerned with partnership between England and Holland since the days of the Glorious Revolution — partnership in peace and in war. It is my task to shed light upon this theme in a very eventful period of the history of our two countries, extending from the period of the Napoleonic wars in Europe to the epoch of modern imperialism, when the European nations divided the world among themselves and conquered large colonial empires in 'a fit of absence of mind', in the words of Seeley, the British historian. This was a period in which the balance of power between the two countries radically changed. For Holland, the nineteenth century meant a loss of prestige and power, reduced as the country was to the status of a small and powerless state, especially after the successful Belgian Revolt of 1830. Britain, on the other hand, had already in the eighteenth century attained absolute naval superiority and global pre-eminence in trade. In the first half of the nineteenth century the conquest of India, and in the second half a new wave of territorial expansion in Africa were added to this. What could partnership possibly mean in this situation of shifting balance of power? There was at least one interesting complicating factor — the vast colonial empire of the Dutch in South-east Asia, which they were able to steer safely through the turmoil of the modern era into the twentieth century. Therefore, I will consider here the question of partnership from the colonial point of view. What can we learn about the history of the two countries and the relationship between them from a colonial perspective?

The unfortunate outcome of Valckenaar's attempts to save the Dutch maritime empire and reconstruct its defences emphasises once more the carelessness and impotence that were characteristic of the Dutch trading empire in its declining days — the days of Apollonius Schotte and Jan Pietersz. Coen had gone indeed. These national figures had always advocated the use of violence to support and protect trade. In their eyes, trade and warfare were inseparable. But this applied no longer to Dutch trade in Asia at the end of the eighteenth century. The power base of the empire weakened with each year. An increasing number of rivals penetrated into the waters of the Archipelago and cast a covetous eye upon even the holiest of the Dutch possessions, the Moluccas, where they had held a monopoly for so long. Profits dwindled, debts piled up, and thus no money was left for purposes of defence or for arms, ammunition, men and ships. The factories and settlements in both the East and the West Indies remained virtually without defence. Occasionally, naval squadrons were dispatched from Holland to put up a show of strength, as, for example, under Van Braam in 1784. For soldiers and other personnel, one was dependent upon the recruitment of indigenous men, be they free blacks in Surinam, or Amboinese, Buginese, Madurese and Javanese in the Archipelago. For arms, munitions and fortifications, no money had been reserved, so that buildings and equipment gradually deteriorated. The Company in Asia took refuge in a policy of cautious and prudent neutrality mingled with a short burst of offensive action now and then.

The change of power in 1795 ushered in a new era in the colonies. French forces invaded Holland and brought about a political revolution which led to the expulsion of the House of Orange to England and the assumption of power by the pro-French patriot movement. It took the Dutch in the colonial settlements quite some time to realise what had happened in Europe and what might be the consequences for the colonies. France was the new ally; radical patriots, who were bound to reform the much criticised colonial administration and trade, were in power in Holland; and England was the enemy who would certainly not tolerate French occupation of the Dutch colonies overseas, and would prevent it by using its already overwhelming naval superiority. In short, war seemed inevitable. The Dutch in South-east Asia had only one man-of-war at their disposal; the number of European soldiers was negligible. The recruitment of an increasing number of Asian soldiers, including the Chinese from Batavia, was necessary to solve the manpower problem. Slaves were called up for military service. These were no more than panicky reactions to the hopeless state of the colonial defences.[9]

We should realise that many did not even want to defend the colonies against Britain. The planters of Surinam, about whom I have already spoken, deliberately sabotaged all defence plans and welcomed an English takeover. They were concerned in the first place with the undisturbed survival of the colonial *ancien régime*. This might not be guaranteed under the French or Dutch patriots, since they were certain to carry out reforms. And Surinam was no exception. The population and government of another Dutch colony in the West, Curaçao, also tried hard to keep the French at arm's length. When, in September 1800, an English man-of-war appeared before Willemstad, the authorities decided at once to seize the opportunity to surrender to the captain of the ship and to accept English dominance. British reinforcements were asked for and soon these were firmly established on the island. Governor Dacres reported later, in 1807, to London: 'No colony in His Majesty's dominions will be more happy than the island of Curaçao'.[10]

William V did everything from his place of exile, Kew, to foster pro-English sentiments in the Dutch colonies. On 7 September 1795 he dispatched his famous Kew letters to the colonial governors, trying to persuade them to surrender to Britain. He urged them: '. . . to consider British forces and warships which will arrive in the colony as forces and ships of a power which is our friend and ally, which comes to save the colony from French occupation'.[11] These letters exercised but little influence. The economic élite of the colonies had its own ideas about the future and if these involved surrendering to the English, this was simply and solely for economic reasons. In Holland, however, the letters caused a great stir and much indignation. Two Leiden professors, Batavus Voorda and Johan Valckenaar, who was a professor at Leiden University before being appointed ambassador in Spain, were commissioned to investigate the matter and advise on whether the letters were to be considered as evidence of high treason, and if so, on how the Prince of Orange might be prosecuted. They concluded that it was, in fact, a case of high treason, but as to prosecution, they could not decide what court or tribunal was qualified enough to judge the case; so the affair petered out.

In the Archipelago, in Batavia, an anti-French mood also prevailed, despite the commercial rivalry between Britain and Holland and the increasing penetration of the Eastern Seas by British ships. When, in 1803, a small French support force arrived in Batavia as a successor to Valckenaar's ill-fated expedition, the French soldiers were pestered to such an extent that they soon returned home. Anti-French feelings also persisted in the reign of Holland's first king, Louis Napoleon, after 1806, despite the fact that he sincerely tried to improve conditions in the colony. This is evident from the notorious toast to the king: 'Damn the King!' by the secretary of the High Government, Moorrees.[12]

It was during Louis's brief reign, however, that a heroic attempt was made to guarantee the safety of Java through the appointment of the skilful and energetic Field-Marshal, Herman Daendels, as Lieutenant-Governor-General in 1808. Some of his decisions with regard to the island's defence were to be of lasting importance throughout the nineteenth century. He decided to abandon the remainder of the Archipelago and concentrate on Java. He constructed the *grote postweg*, a new road along the north coast of Java, to facilitate troop movement and improve communications on the island — still for the most part inaccessible. Daendels preferred to defend Java from the interior in the rugged mountain ranges of the western and central areas, from which the colonial army might launch a kind of guerilla campaign against the invading British. First, the British army was to be kept occupied in the swampy and coastal lowlands, where the landing and manoeuvring of large forces were difficult, and where many would die of disease and exhaustion. Then the weakened forces were to be lured into the mountainous interior, where the Dutch would have the opportunity to deal with them, benefiting from their own superior knowledge of the terrain — in short, a war of attrition. Daendels realised, however, that his plans would for the time being, be a mere 'castle in Spain', to use an appropriate metaphor, owing to lack of money, means and, above all, time. Therefore, he concentrated upon West Java alone, though explicitly not upon Batavia, which would be left at the enemy's mercy; nothing could illustrate better the change of conception from maritime to territorial defence which was brought about by Daendels. Batavia's walls and castle were demolished and the few remaining batteries were left in the hands of the Chinese. Buitenzorg, further inland, was viewed as the new defence centre, with Meester Cornelis, halfway between Batavia and Buitenzorg, as a military outpost. At the end of Daendels's term, only Meester Cornelis was strong enough to face the enemy.

Daendels also reorganised the armed forces. The numbers were raised to 18,000, of whom 7 per cent were Europeans. The number of officers was increased through haphazard promotion of seamen, cobblers and other useful craftsmen of European origin. Most of them lacked military training or skills, and were ignorant of the Malay language, and some of them were even unable to write their names. As for the indigenous recruits, most of them arrived in chains. Dayak soldiers from Borneo were handcuffed upon arrival, being supplied by the Sultan of Banjarmasin, who received a payment for each recruit.[13]

The long-expected attack was finally launched in August 1811; it came, not under Daendels's governorship — he was discharged by Napoleon — but under Jan Willem Janssens, who was assisted by the French general, Jumel, and 500 French troops. The expedition, prepared with meticulous care by Raffles, comprised more than 12,000 men, half of them European and half Indian, commanded by Sir Samuel Auchmuty and personally supervised by Lord Minto, the Governor of British India. Without meeting any resistance they advanced to Meester Cornelis, where the offensive came to a temporary standstill. Soon, however, they discovered the enemy's weak spot, assisted by a deserting sergeant, and succeeded in capturing the fortress in the space of three hours, and in subsequently dislodging the Dutch from this stronghold. The Dutch suffered 2,000 casualties, and another 6,000 were taken prisoner; British losses numbered 900. The poor quality of the troops, bad leadership and misunderstandings among the officers, and large-scale desertion among the indigenous soldiers were the main factors responsible for this ignominious defeat.[14] Raffles was appointed the new Governor of Java and its dependencies. With his unbridled energy and organisational genius, he implemented important reforms and innovations in the fields of administration and taxation. His brief reign resulted in a totally changed view of Java and its importance, from which the Dutch were soon to benefit.

Britain had finally conquered the Dutch colonial settlements, and these were now British property by right of conquest. Seen from the perspective of the period, this meant that for Holland, if it was ever to revive as an independent nation, the era of colonial expansion was over. There seemed to be no chance of regaining the former colonial status.

But, as it happened, South-east Asia was restored to the Dutch rather soon: in 1814 by convention, and in 1816 in reality. Now the Dutch had to think anew about the administration and defence of the Archipelago, and set up an army and navy.

What was the military heritage of the years of war with Britain between 1795 and 1814? To my mind this heritage was twofold.

Firstly, as the outcome of the occurrences of those years, the conclusion was drawn that the Archipelago or even just Java, was, in fact, indefensible. This notion became part of the Dutch colonial conscious-ness more strongly and persistently than before, and not only among Dutch politicians (who always complain about the expenses of armies and arms), but equally among the colonial military themselves. The year 1811 proved that a successful defence of Java was highly doubtful. It also demonstrated that the use of indigenous troops — which remained absolutely essential throughout the rest of the nineteenth century — was an additional source of uncertainty. Colonial defences therefore proved a dual problem: a problem of availability of men and means; and a problem of the reliability of indigenous soldiers. It was a complicated situation in which the Dutch found themselves after 1816.

Secondly, the Dutch drew the conclusion that if they were to defend the East Indies against a foreign attack once more, this should be done in Java, and from a territorial perspective. The role of the navy was played out for the time being. This approach, initiated by Daendels, was continued by Van den Bosch after 1830, and was to remain the guiding principle of the authorities during the rest of the nineteenth century up to 1892.[15]

Under the convention of 1814 the Indonesian Archipelago, Surinam and the Antilles were restored to the Dutch, owing to the policy of Britain which aimed at creating a strong Dutch buffer state in the North Sea area to check French expansion. In fact, the new state (including its colonial possessions) was 'made in England'. This national revival ushered in an era of warm co-operation between our two countries, a 'special relationship', as it was recently described in an admirable book by the Dutch historian, Van Sas.[16] In South-east Asia, however, there were no signs of any special relationship. Raffles and his successor, John Fendall, were not favourably disposed towards the returning Dutch. Soon after his appointment Raffles wrote to Bengal: 'The annexation of Java to our Indian empire opens to the English nation views of so enlarged a nature as to seem equally to demand and justify a bolder policy than we could have lately contemplated'.[17] He also kept harping on about the humanitarian argument: 'Our aim is not that of the extension of territory for the sake of dominion nor that of monopoly for the sake of universal exclusion, but that of superior influence . . . which may check piracies, regulate trade and effect the general ends of civilisation'.[18] His real aims, however, were far from being humanitarian. Until the very end of his governorship he tried to undermine Dutch influence as much as possible. As late as 1814 he still tried to gain control of Sumatra and Bali in an attempt to encircle Java with British settlements: 'A chain of posts which would prevent the enemy from attaining very formidable power or deriving his former advantages from the possession of Java',[19] he wrote to the directors of the British East India Company. From the beginning, however, the directors resisted Raffles's attempts to extend British influence. They had a feeling that they were being forced into Java, which would entail more problems and more expenses. They advised the Cabinet negatively with regard to Java, with the backing of Lord Castlereagh, who said, 'To take this possession, much cherished by the Dutch nation, would be prejudicial to Orange interests and discreditable to the British character'.[20]

The British still held a bridgehead in the Archipelago after 1816 — Bencoolen in West Sumatra, with Raffles as its director. He made frantic efforts to set up 'a shop next door', as he called it. But his Sumatra policy, too, turned out to be a failure between 1816 and 1825. 'Mr. Raffles is a gentleman in charge of a subordinate commercial factory', the directors wrote, 'and, however individually respectable, he has in so many instances over-stepped the limits of his duty'.[21] However, in one respect his policy was extremely successful, namely, in the foundation of Singapore in 1819, in territory claimed by the Dutch. 'With this single action alone I would undertake to counteract all the plans of *Mijnheer*. It breaks the spell. And they are no longer the exclusive sovereigns of the Eastern Seas',[22] he said. Despite initial criticism, London accepted the foundation of the new settlement, because it recognised Singapore's enormous strategic and commercial potential. Dutch protests, which continued for years, were ignored. The Dutch eventually accepted the fact that Singapore was and would remain British in the Treaty of 1824.

So, in the East, instead of a special relationship, the old colonial suspicion and rivalry returned after 1816. But this renewed rivalry posed no threat to the special relationship in Europe. The Dutch accepted their new colonial task with enthusiasm and looked upon themselves as the natural and sole heirs to the Archipelago, without realising, it seems, that they had received it back out of British hands. Self-confidently, they introduced a neo-mercantilist trade policy and levied severely high import taxes upon British textiles, against which Raffles and the merchants of Singapore protested. But the British Cabinet was not impressed, either by Dutch policy, or by the merchant protests. It firmly stuck to a pro-Dutch line based on harsh reality. A cabinet memorandum said: 'The Dutch are dependent upon British support and could never in the long run constitute a serious threat to British commercial interests in Southeast Asia'.[23] For the remainder of the nineteenth century, the Anglo-Dutch trade conflict flared up time and again. British traders, among them many Chinese and Malays, regularly protested against Dutch restrictive measures, but were only hesitantly and reluctantly supported in this by the British Government. London did not want to create a diplomatic conflict, or worse, over trading interests. When the Dutch finally began to liberalise their trade by introducing new tariffs in the 1860s, the British reacted favourably. They praised the Dutch for creating better conditions for friendship. The Dutch themselves understood the importance of a more liberal trade policy: colonial minister De Waal told Parliament in 1871 that 'a liberal trade policy in our possessions will constitute an essential contribution to the defence of our territory against a foreign enemy'.[24]

The leading principle of British policy with regard to South-east Asia was not protection of its trade, but safeguarding of its strategic position in the Far East. Hence reasons of security dictated Britain's attitude towards the Netherlands Indies. Britain was only interested in those parts of the Archipelago that were of strategic importance: North and East Sumatra (i.e., Aceh and Siak), because of their command of the Straits of Malacca, and the West Coast of Borneo, because of its control of the route to China. It did not wish the Dutch to possess exclusive dominance over these areas. If necessary, Britain was to have the freedom to intervene. This explains the recurrent diplomatic conflict over Sumatra and Borneo between Britain and the Netherlands after 1830. The contest for political dominance continued until 1871 for Sumatra, and until 1888 for Borneo, with the Siak Treaty of the former year and the establishment of the British Protectorate in 1888 finally putting an end to the struggle. In this protracted colonial conflict the London Treaty of 1824 played a crucial role. There was a misunderstanding on the part of the Dutch about its meaning. It recognised Singapore, the former Dutch factories in India, and Malacca, as British territory, and Bencoolen and Biliton as Dutch. The Dutch were under the impression that it had settled the territorial boundaries once and for all, and excluded 'common property' in the Archipelago. This interpretation was not accepted by the British, who firmly intended to keep a finger in the pie in Sumatra and Borneo, which was facilitated by the fact that neither Aceh nor Borneo were even mentioned in the text of the treaty. This rendered Dutch claims particularly weak.

Apart from this misinterpretation of the Treaty of 1824, one more factor which tended to make the Dutch more dependent on the British was the military situation in the Netherlands Indies. The Treaty of 1824 had come just in time. The following year saw the outbreak of the Java War which had disastrous consequences for the Dutch. Thousands of extra soldiers were sent to Java, tens of thousands of indigenous soldiers and auxiliary troops were recruited, and Dutch garrisons in other islands were stripped of their men; yet, despite all this, the war could only be brought to a successful end after five years of bitter fighting. This did not escape the attention of the English; a British trader wrote home that 'the Dutch have not only not force enough to be assailants, but even to act on the defensive and afford protection to their own territories'.[25] Foreign Minister Verstolk van Soelen drew the same conclusion, reporting to the king that 'we are too weak to protect ourselves; an alliance with Britain would be logical, but too expensive in terms of men and means. We cannot afford such an expensive policy; therefore, the best thing to do is to pursue a policy of isolation. When we are in danger, Britain will come and rescue us automatically'.[26]

This latter expectation may have been justified when Verstolk made his statement, in 1829, but probably was not after 1830. British acceptance and support of the Belgian revolt as a *fait accompli* after that year shocked the Dutch. All of a sudden they felt less confident about themselves and their colonial possessions.

Under the impact of this experience Dutch politicians for a while showed an interest in problems of colonial defence. In 1834, General Van der Wijck presented a major blueprint for the defence of Java. A supposed new English campaign against Java served as a basis for the plan. Like Daendels, Van der Wijck started from the assumption that Java would be defended internally by an army trained in mobile warfare and guerilla tactics. The capital and administrative centre was to be transferred from Batavia to a location further inland. Although this plan was approved by the government, it took no decision about the transfer of the capital. King William I, who actively participated in the debate, remarkably enough suggested Bandung as the new capital and centre of defence. But it was this issue of the new location of the capital, along with continued arguing about a new naval base and the role of the navy, which caused a delay in the execution and eventually total abandonment of the plan. As a result, the subject of colonial defence almost wholly disappeared from public debate and the decision-making process until the end of the nineteenth century. After the 1830s, there seems to have been hardly any further serious thinking about colonial defence. The alternative to a military approach was, in the words of former Minister and Member of Parliament, Elout, 'a policy of independence, neutrality, careful protection against foreign intrusion, and painstaking non-intervention in the affairs of other nations'.[27] These principles determined the Dutch attitude towards England, and were consistently put into practice for the remainder of the century — according to the Dutch themselves, with considerable success. They felt increasingly more confident about the results of this policy. 'A foreign enemy who might attack us is a thing of the past', said one author in a colonial journal, 'the very idea is a museum piece; it is one of the myths of colonial policy'.[28] Governor-General Van Lansberge even felt that all money spent on defence against a foreign European enemy was a waste.[29] This policy of neutrality and good behaviour constituted the Dutch way of participating in colonial power politics. It was based upon a realistic assessment of their own military impotence. This was the way to deal with a powerful neighbour, to avert threats and to make sure of assistance in case of emergency. It was, in fact, a remarkable attempt to transform dependence into power, weakness into strength.

The success of this policy depended on diplomacy. With regard to the contest for Sumatra and Borneo, Dutch diplomatic activity was persistent and unyielding, and met with success in the case of Sumatra. In other matters it was more yielding and less persistent. This was the case, for example, with regard to the recruitment of Negro soldiers in West Africa. From 1837 onwards, many recruits from the Gold Coast went to the Netherlands Indies to serve in the colonial army. At the beginning of the 1840s the British Government suddenly raised objections to this practice, as it considered it a form of slave trade in disguise. Under the increasing pressure of the British, the Dutch finally gave up their recruitment activities here, although this was a matter of great importance for the colonial army. The decision was based entirely upon political grounds. Anglo-Dutch relations were already at a low point because of the arrival and settlement of James Brooke in Borneo; another conflict would harm the precarious relationship even further. When the Dutch Government tried to revive recruitment in various countries of Africa in the 1870s and 1880s, the plan was soon abandoned altogether, on account of rising political tension with regard to British interests in Borneo.[30]

The Dutch tried to settle colonial conflicts or rather, to prevent such conflicts from arising through their envoy in London. In the Borneo and

Sumatra affairs, the envoy played a key role in the negotiations, through regular discussions with officials of the Foreign and Colonial Secretaries in London. His role seemed to be vital in the efforts to safeguard the security of the Netherlands Indies and to enlist British support against all kinds of foreign intrusions. The Dutch were bound hand and foot to the British with respect to these issues. To a large extent this was the result of the Treaty of 1824, especially its third article, which stipulated that the Dutch Government was under an obligation to inform the British of all contracts and treaties concluded between the Netherlands and the Indonesian princes. A constant flow of information thus went from the Dutch Ministries for Colonial and Foreign Affairs through the Dutch legation in London to the British Foreign Office. From the diplomatic correspondence in the archives, it can be concluded that this transfer of information was carried out very reluctantly and with much delay in the first half of the nineteenth century and the 1850s and 1860s. After the treaty of 1871 and the outbreak of the Aceh war it became a more complete and regular communication. By then even the smallest supplementary contracts and the most petty details were mentioned to the British.

The success or failure of Dutch diplomatic intervention in matters of the colonies depended upon a number of factors, among which were the policy of the Dutch cabinets and the instructions issued to the envoy in London, the envoy's knowledge of colonial matters, his diplomatic qualities and personality. On each of these much more could be said than is possible within the narrow limits of this article. As to the first aspects, those of the cabinet policy and instructions to the envoy, it is clear that the Dutch cabinets always realised that the Netherlands did not possess any real authority in the Archipelago as a whole, although the Dutch persisted in pretending that the Archipelago was Dutch territory.

When the Dutch Colonial Administration in 1841 raised the alarm on account of mass importation of false coins into Sumatra by British traders from Birmingham, the Dutch Cabinet refused to go into action. J. C. Baud, the Minister for the Colonies, argued that it was impossible to stop the importation 'because the island of Sumatra does not wholly belong to us'. Only once the Dutch envoy, Dedel, protested against it in a letter to Lord Aberdeen, the British Secretary for Foreign Affairs; the protest was rejected bluntly: there was no 'sufficient evidence to warrant the prosecution'.[31] The importation continued unhampered until the end of the 1850s without further Dutch attempts to stop it.

In the 1840s much more serious trouble arose about the settlement of James Brooke in North Borneo and the British claims on the island of Labuan just off the coast of Borneo. It is too well known from the books of Irwin and others to be retold here.[32] But with respect to Dutch policy, it is interesting to quote from a report to the king in November 1845. 'It is true', it was said, 'that neither the Dutch East India Company nor the present Dutch Administration have ever exercised any sovereign rights in this part of Borneo or on the island of Labuan'.[33] And it was also admitted by the authors of the report that the Treaty of 1824 did not offer any protection against British claims on Borneo or any other part of the Archipelago where the Dutch Administration was not firmly established. More than ever before, the text of this treaty was deplored in the 1840s, when the Borneo issue and the threat of an English intervention simply overshadowed all other colonial issues. The Dutch line of conduct *vis-à-vis* the British can be summarised as follows: to persuade the British Cabinet to be careful and not spoil the good relationship between the two countries by ill-considered actions in Borneo or elsewhere, and keep in mind 'the spirit and the meaning of the negotiations of the years between 1817 and 1824 and of the Treaty . . .'[34] Or, as Minister for the Colonies, Baud, put it in even more plain terms: 'If all means of persuasion and diplomacy fail, we will end up with being dependent upon "the wisdom of the British Cabinet in not exercising in practice the rights it reserves for itself"'.[35] In short, the Dutch Government fully realised (1) That the final decisions about the actual limits of colonial policy and territorial expansion were taken in London, and (2) That it was able to influence this only to a very limited extent.

This was proved once again by further developments in Borneo in the 1840s, and again in the 1870s and 1880s. In reply to Dutch protests against further encroachments in Borneo, Lord Aberdeen, Secretary for Foreign Affairs, argued in December 1845 that the Netherlands 'has not hesitated to extend its political relations in this and other portions of the Indian Archipelago as are not by the Treaty of 1824 included among those within which no Netherland settlement can be formed'.[36] According to him the Netherlands had no right to blame the British; the Dutch themselves were the cause 'of much unpleasant discussion', because of their 'restrictive commercial policy' and 'undue interference . . . with Mr. Brooke's legitimate objects and pursuits'.[37] And he added: 'Please be so kind as to keep in mind "the high character of that gentleman", who is continuously concerned for the "furtherance of civilisation, the discouragement of piratical pursuits, and the promotion of the welfare of the native population"'.[38] As if he wanted to say: 'This cannot be said of the Dutch, so keep quiet!' Thus the Dutch envoy, Dedel, returned empty-handed and the Dutch could only hope for the best.

Even more relentless was the way in which Lord Salisbury dealt with the Dutch envoy, Van Bylandt, when the British interference with Borneo became a hot issue once more in the 1870s. The Dutch tried to prevent the settlement of the trading house of Dent and Overbeek, and a possible British protectorate in North Borneo. Van Bylandt, more impatient and dynamic than his predecessors, told the British plainly that the area they claimed did in fact fall under Dutch sovereignty. Lord Salisbury, the Secretary for Foreign Affairs, was not really impressed by the envoy's statement, and in the Dutch Cabinet it caused a considerable stir. Van Bylandt was immediately reprimanded by the Minister for Foreign Affairs, who repeated the time-honoured point of view that the Netherlands had no rights in the area whatsoever. In his zeal to defend the Dutch cause, Van Bylandt had also said that the British should refrain from settling in Borneo, as the Netherlands in its turn did not attempt to settle in Australia! Salisbury's only reaction to this was a laugh. Van Bylandt understood, as he wrote to the Minister, that the British were not willing to 'recognise the equality of rights between a large and a small nation'. He got the strong impression that the establishment of British sovereignty in Borneo was only a matter of time. It was, indeed, to materialise soon, in 1888, when the British proclaimed a protectorate over the northern part of the island.[39]

As to the extension of their authority and political influence in the Archipelago, the Dutch cabinets knew how powerless they in fact were. Via the envoys in London, they did their utmost on the one hand to obtain British support and ask for assistance against other nations who might ever try to capture parts of it, and simultaneously, on the other hand, to keep the British out of the Archipelago. Every envoy responded in his own way, and with more or less luck and success, to this challenge. The ways in which the Dutch envoys in London had to manage the colonial relationship with the British deserves much closer attention in the future, and more archival research should be carried out.

It is striking to see that in a number of cases both clear instructions and knowledge about colonial afairs were lacking in the legation. When a conflict broke out on the Dutch treaty with Bali, concluded by General Van Swieten in 1849 after the third military expedition, the Dutch envoy, Schimmelpenninck, got into difficulties. He had not received a copy of the treaty nor any instructions, and he thus had to enter, almost unprepared, an interview with Lord Palmerston, the successor to Lord Aberdeen. No wonder that he blundered. He referred to the British conquest of Punjab 'as affording a precedent and a justification for measures of aggrandisement resorted to by any other Power for the protection of its own frontier'.[40] This resulted in a sharp reprimand. 'England', said Palmerston, 'is free to do what it likes in India, because there is no treaty with a third party. But the Netherlands Government is fettered in its action in regard to these Indian states by its Treaty engagements with Great Britain'; namely, through the Treaty of 1824.[41] And furthermore, Punjabi forces attacked the British territories first, but 'it was the Government of the Netherlands that invaded the territory of Bali' without 'a just cause of war'.[42] And he asked: 'Was it necessary for the future security of Java' to attack the princes of Bali?[43] By saying this he implicitly demonstrated the British views: Java was seen as indisputably Dutch, but the rest of the Archipelago was not. It was a Dutch 'sphere of influence' at best — not a territory in which the supreme authority of the Dutch was fully recognised. This was 1851 and it exposed the shaky foundations of the Dutch empire in the East: unable to set up its authority in the area as a whole by conquest and force, chained to John Bull for military and political support, and simultaneously afraid that England might seize large portions of Borneo and Sumatra.

In the 1870s we still find the same situation. In the Dent and Overbeek affair on Borneo, envoy Van Bylandt received instructions only after two and a half years. In the meantime he had to protect the Dutch interests in contacts with officials of the Foreign Office on his own initiative. In his correspondence he criticises the lack of precise instructions, the slow policy of the Ministry, the lack of any response to information sent to the Hague, and above all the practice of protesting and intervening with the British only by means of verbal communications and informal statements. 'During the eight and a half years of my envoyship your [Minister of Foreign Affairs] dépêche of 11 November, 1879 (on Borneo) was the first one I ever had to read to the British Government and leave behind'. And, he says, 'Only written statements are seriously dealt with'; all the rest, verbal statements, protests, informal letters, etc. are simply ignored.[44]

It is too early to give a definite assessment of Dutch diplomacy in the Anglo-Dutch colonial relationship. But it seems reasonable to say that political and diplomatic procedures were often slow, lacking precise and timely response; even in important, and (for the Dutch colonial administration and territory) crucial cases, the envoys in London did not receive accurate instructions or information which would have made it possible for them to anticipate. This is to be explained, not by referring to neutrality, moral superiority, legalism and anti-militarism, which are often considered characteristic of Dutch foreign policy,[45] but primarily by pointing to two mutually reinforcing factors: (1) The general indifference towards the colonies, combined with the unwillingness to spend money on them (even when there was, in the second half of the nineteenth century, plenty of money available through the immense profits from Java), and (2) The paralysing effect of the consciousness (widespread in Dutch political circles) of military impotence and absolute political dependence on Great Britain. The 'effective occupation' of the Archipelago was only to be achieved by British political support, and would succeed as far as the British would like it to succeed. Dutch cabinets knew this and behaved accordingly. Geographically, the Dutch colonial territories might be immense; politically, however, Dutch colonialism in the international context was as dwarf-like as the Dutch state was in European politics.

This chapter has presented a bird's-eye view of Anglo-Dutch relations in the colonies. At the end of the eighteenth century the presence of the European powers in Asia became more conspicuous. As the trading companies lost their importance, the European states stepped in and clashed with one another. England especially, with its superior naval forces, gained pre-eminence in Asian waters. The Dutch reacted to this by adopting a cautious policy of armed neutrality. The populations of the Dutch colonies were overtly pro-English. Britain's power reached its zenith with the conquest of Java in 1811. It looked as if the era of Dutch colonialism was over. Because of British dominance in European politics and their wish to maintain the existing balance of power with the help of a strong and enlarged Kingdom of the Netherlands under the House of Orange, part of the former Dutch colonies were restored. Now the second era of Dutch colonial expansion began, but what a different one from the first! No longer was a trading empire set up on the basis of the conquests of a band of merchant warriors as in the past, but a territorial sphere of influence had yet to be effectively created by military means and through administrative control. This had to be effected by a country that was not actually up to the task, and it took a century of fighting before the Dutch could call the Archipelago 'the Netherlands East

Indies'. In this process, military interests were continually neglected and made subordinate to political issues. Until the end of the nineteenth century there was no consistent military defence strategy; thinking about this was neglected and left to the frustrated military. Yet the Dutch were obliged to participate in power politics. They did so by adopting a policy which made a virtue of necessity: a policy of non-intervention and good behaviour, which was considered as constituting a defence policy of sorts. This policy was specially adapted to shaping the Dutch colonial relationship with England. From the beginning the defence of the Archipelago was regarded as an impossibility, and the Dutch tacitly relied upon British support. Therefore, to a large extent they were at the mercy of Britain — a circumstance which gave this relationship its ambiguous and unpleasant character. Dutch colonial expansion was partly obstructed by the English desire to control parts of Sumatra and Borneo in order to protect the route to the Far East, and partly supported and encouraged by the British recognition of the Archipelago as a Dutch sphere of influence, and by British assistance to the Dutch in keeping out foreigners. Covered from the rear, as it were, the Dutch were free to extend their influence over the Archipelago in their own good time.

To describe this relationship as a form of partnership seems incorrect. From their former position of Lords of the Eastern Seas the Dutch were reduced to the status of a dependent 'ally of a kind'. The tacit support of Britain was made the cornerstone of Dutch colonial policy. When the age of modern imperialism with its manifold tensions began, the Dutch faced the future of the Netherlands Indies with confidence. With the help of Britain, which was so overtly imperialistic in other parts of the globe, the Netherlands Indies might be safely steered through the vicissitudes of the modern world.

NOTES

1. The text of the treaty of 31 May 1800 between Spain and the Batavian Republic: Algemeen Rijksarchief, The Hague (ARA): *Archief Buitenlandse Zaken vóór 1813*, 422.
2. ARA, Archief Buitenlandse Zaken vóór 1813, 326, where the story of the capture can be found.
3. Quoted in J. A. Sillem, *Het leven van Mr. Johan Valckenaer, 1759-1821* (Amsterdam, 1883), II, p. 121.

4. Sillem, *ibid.*, p. 119.
5. ARA, Archief Buitenlandse Zaken vóór 1813, 326.
6. *Ibid.*
7. *Ibid.*
8. *Ibid.*, Report by the medical officers Reinking and Van Elten.
9. For the military and naval situation after 1795: E. S. van Eyck van Heslinga, *Van compagnie naar koopvaardij. De scheepvaartverbinding van de Bataafse Republiek met de koloniën in Azië, 1795-1806* (Amsterdam, 1988), pp. 72 ff.
10. J. Hartog, *Curaçao, van kolonie tot autonomie. Geschiedenis van de Nederlandse Antillen III* (Oranjestad, 1961), p. 549.
11. Quoted in J. Wolbers, *Geschiedenis van Suriname* (Amsterdam, 1861), pp. 459-60.
12. Van Eyck van Heslinga, *op. cit.*, p. 68.
13. G. Nypels, *Oost-Indische krijgsqeschiedenis. De veroverinq van Java door de Enqelschen in 1811* (Breda, 1895), pp. 5-7.
14. *Ibid.*, p. 19 ff.
15. In 1892 a new system of defence of the Netherlands Indies came about; see G. Teitler, *Anatomie van de Indische defensie. Scenario's, plannen, beleid 1892-1920* (Amsterdam, 1988).
16. N. C. F. van Sas, *Onze natuurlijkste bondgenoot. Nederland, Enqeland en Europa, 1813-1831* (Groningen, 1985).
17. Quoted in J. Bastin, *Essays on Indonesian and Malayan history* (Singapore, 1961), p. 118.
18. *Ibid.*, p. 129.
19. *Ibid.*, p. 115.
20. *Ibid.*, p. 138.
21. J. Bastin, *The British in West Sumatra, 1685-1825. A selection of documents mainly from the East India Company Records* (Kuala Lumpur, 1965), p. 171.
22. Bastin, *Essays*, p. 177.
23. *Ibid.*, p. 178.
24. An., 'De verdediging van Nederlands-Indië tegen een buitenlandschen vijand' *De Indische Gids* 21 (1899), p. 1241.
25. Quoted in V. J. H. Houben, *Kraton en Kumpenie. Surakarta en Yogyakarta 1830-1870* (Diss. Leiden, 1987), p. 12.
26. The memorandum of Minister Verstolk van Soelen (1829) of which this is a summary, in A. Vandenbosch, *Dutch Foreign Policy Since 1815. A Study in Small Power Politics* (The Hague, 1959).
27. P. J. Elout van Soeterwoude, *Bijdragen tot de geschiedenis der onderhandelingen met Engeland 1820-1824* (The Hague, 1863), XXXI.
28. An., *op. cit.*, p. 1242.
29. *Ibid.*, p. 1248.
30. See correspondence of the Dutch envoy, Count Van Bylandt, on this question, in ARA, Legatie-archief Groot Brittannië 1814-1913, 416.
31. Legatie-archief Groot Brittannië, 186.

32. G. Irwin, *Nineteenth-century Borneo. A Study on Diplomatic Rivalry* (The Hague, 1955).
33. Cabinet report to King Willem II, November 1845, Legatie-archief Groot-Brittannië, 187.
34. Legatie-archief, 187.
35. Memorandum of Minister J. C. Baud, 29 December 1846, Legatie-archief, 187.
36. Legatie-archief, 187.
37. *Ibid.*
38. *Ibid.*
39. Count Van Bylandt and Lord Salisbury, correspondence of Van Bylandt, Legatie-archief, 376.
40. Legatie-archief, 188.
41. *Ibid.*
42. *Ibid.*
43. *Ibid.*
44. Legatie-archief, 376.
45. See, for example, J. J. C. Voorhoeve, *Peace, Profits and Principles. A Study of Dutch Foreign Policy* (The Hague, 1979), pp. 49 ff. As I see it, the tradition of moral superiority, legalism and pacifism became an integral part of Dutch foreign policy only in the twentieth century.

5

ANGLO-DUTCH RELATIONS, 1936–1988. COLONIAL AND EUROPEAN TRENDS

G. Teitler

In 1936 the government of the Netherlands decided to send a naval attaché to its embassy in London. The predecessor of this officer had been recalled in the early 1920s. At that time there was nothing to indicate that there would be war or an international crisis, while the armed forces in the Netherlands had little money to spend. Things looked very different in 1936. The decision to send naval and military attachés abroad reflected an awareness of increased international tensions. That the first attaché was sent to London is significant in this respect.

However, the new naval attaché owed his appointment not solely to the fear of the Germans. As to Europe, the Netherlands hoped that the international situation would not deteriorate beyond the 1913 point. A balance of power prevailed, thanks to which the Netherlands hoped to maintain its neutrality. However, that balance was missing in the Far East. Just to keep it in Europe and the Middle East, Great Britain had no choice but to neglect it around Singapore. In this respect the Netherlands had growing doubts about its neutrality in Asia. There the Dutch were confronted with two problems. First, how to get the most out of their defence investments. Second, to what extent were the British willing and able to send military help during a crisis. As for the first problem, the Royal Netherlands Navy was assigned the task of keeping the Dutch East Indies out of any war. The Dutch colonial army, however, refused to accept this naval superiority. They hoped to match the reach and mobility of the navy by acquiring medium bombers. As these aeroplanes were intended to attack enemy warships, a major interservice rivalry developed among the Dutch.[1] To solve this problem they looked to the British. Prime Minister Hendrik Colijn even stated, 'My choice must depend on what I think or know England would prefer me to do'.[2] The naval attaché too was busy asking the British their opinion on colonial defence. What would be the impact of bombers or cruisers on an enemy who, by force of circumstance, had to come by sea?[3] As a matter of fact, Colijn and the attaché received rather contradictory advice from their contacts in Britain. But, as the air versus sea power competition was still raging in Great Britain, this came as no surprise. Eventually, the British Chiefs of Staff declared that for the Dutch the best thing to do was to rely mainly on shore-based bombers. The Royal Netherlands Navy should concentrate on submarines, mines and motor torpedo-boats, and should aspire to defend only local areas. As to the bomber force, they pointed out that at the outbreak of hostilities British aircraft might be stationed at airfields in the East Indies. In that case Anglo-Dutch co-operation would be greatly helped if the aircraft of the Dutch colonial army were similar to the types operated by the Royal Air Force.[4] These views clearly indicate that the British did not make a push for a powerful Dutch fleet in the Far East. In this respect British policy was remarkably consistent. Just before the outbreak of the First World War, when such a fleet seemed to be a strong option, Churchill, then First Lord of the Admiralty, announced that this would be against British interests. He feared that in the end a Dutch fleet might come under the influence of the Germans, even if it were built for use in the Dutch East Indies.[5] After the defeat of Germany in 1918, British views remained the same, although there were no plans for the building of a Dutch war fleet at that time. The British explicitly told the Dutch naval attaché in London that they very much preferred to keep it that way. The attaché noted that the British were not inclined to see a Dutch fleet as a purely colonial force; any Dutch fleet would be attached to the coastline of the Netherlands in Europe. In British opinion, colonial defence was clearly something that small nations should leave to powerful and friendly neighbours.[6] This paternalistic view had evaporated fifteen years later, but still, the British hoped that the Royal Netherlands Navy in the Far East would concentrate on local defence. Only then could they be certain that the main part of that Navy would not fall into German hands. The aforementioned views of the British Chiefs of Staff were eventually not presented to the Dutch. On the one hand, the British, especially the military, were reluctant to give the Dutch any hope of spontaneous assistance in times of crisis. After all, British military power was subject to great pressure already, while the defence of Great Britain took precedence over the security of Singapore. On the other hand, the government of the Netherlands was not yet willing to enter into formal negotiations with Great Britain. They hoped that Japan could perhaps still be contained by diplomatic and economic means. The naval attaché, Lieutenant-Commander De Booy, reported that his military contacts in London were deeply concerned about their present inability to reinforce the Far East.[7] He warned the Hague that it would be wrong to count on spontaneous British help in times of crisis.[8] Even staff talks with the Dutch were not held for the moment. The informal exchange of technical information at the attaché level was the limit of British intrepidity. Somewhat embarrassed, De Booy noted that even at this modest level the British still had a lot to learn about the Dutch armed forces. When he was asked to correct the proofs of the 1936 edition of the authoritative *Jane's Fighting Ships*, he was painfully surprised at the rather enormous number of mistakes in the pages devoted to the Royal Netherlands Navy.[9] The Dutch hoped to remain neutral. The British hoped that they would not be challenged in the Far East and be forced to come to the rescue of the Dutch East Indies. More and more officers visited each other's colonies, but they only exchanged information.[10] And even in this respect De Booy had to learn that there were limits to British co-operation. When he heard about Asdic he predicted a rapid decline in importance for submarines. He was very pessimistic, however, about the chances of obtaining Asdic sets for the Royal Netherlands Navy, which was still short of an adequate number of them. But he thought that this was probably not the real reason for the reluctance to discuss a possible transfer. The British simply did not trust the Dutch to keep the Asdic secret under cover, although De Booy assured his superiors that this mistrust was not related to the Royal Netherlands Navy. It was Dutch industry the British felt suspicious of, probably because of its ties to German industry.[11]

Shortly after the Germans invaded the Netherlands the Royal Family and the Cabinet fled to Great Britain. So did a considerable part of the Royal Netherlands Navy. They refused to surrender and followed their queen and government into exile. After the inevitable delay caused by disarray and confusion, this part of the Royal Netherlands Navy was admitted into the Royal Navy.[12] In the Far East too, Anglo-Dutch co-operation increased. The British government still refused to commit itself to the defence of the Dutch East Indies, but the exchange of information intensified, while, in the first months of 1941, several British-Dutch-Australian conferences were held. At first the United States only sent observers to these meetings. Soon they were allowed to participate actively. By that time, liaison officers had already been exchanged between Singapore and Batavia. Parallel to these developments, the American president and the British Prime Minister decided on a policy of 'Germany First', in case the United States should become involved in the war, and Japan chose to carry out an attack in the Pacific.[13] This implied that it was up to the Singapore conferences to design strategies for the defence of the Pacific.[14] Gradually it was accepted during these meetings that a major Japanese attack was within the bounds of possibility. Still, it was thought to be unlikely that Japan was strong enough to launch a campaign against both the British and the Dutch possessions. After all, a considerable number of Japanese troops were still tied down in China, while the danger of American intervention likewise forced them to withhold reserves from an all-out attack.

Of course, to the British, the defence of Singapore was of the utmost importance. The Dutch were inclined to accept this priority, yet they succeeded in drawing British attention to the Dutch East Indies' islands east of Singapore. Not surprisingly, the Australians and Americans also warned about the fact that the Japanese were advancing to the east. In the end, Dutch bomber and fighter squadrons were earmarked for action over Singapore and Malaya. Dutch cruisers and submarines were detailed for their defence, while Australian bombers and troops were committed to defend the islands of Amboina and Timor, both situated to the south of the Philippines. A Dutch proposal to form an international naval squadron was turned down, however, by the British. In their opinion, a squadron without battleships would be no match for the Japanese.

These arrangements were not politically binding. Nevertheless, when the Japanese mounted the attack, they formed the basis of the allied defence of Malaya, Singapore and the Dutch East Indies. An international naval squadron was eventually formed, but only after the *Repulse* and the *Prince of Wales* had been sunk. After the dissolution of the ABDA command, Anglo-Dutch co-operation did not slacken. Again, the most important developments took place in the Far East. The 'Germany First' policy meant that the Netherlands could contribute very little to the fighting in Europe. Warships, planes and so on could be obtained from the British allies. All manpower, however, had to come from the Netherlands, and its geographical position ruled out an early liberation.[15] This left the war against Japan as the only activity to which the Dutch could make a substantial contribution. Several factors complicated this situation. First, the line separating the British and American command zones in the Far East ran straight through the Dutch East Indies.[16] Second, even before the Japanese took Java it had been decided to establish an integrated command on Ceylon for all Dutch and Dutch colonial forces in the Far East that managed to avoid captivity.[17] By choosing Ceylon, the Netherlands government in exile indicated that it was quite content to remain in the British sphere of influence. After all, the British host was as eager to get back its colonial possessions as the exiles themselves.

As the American military preponderance grew, however, this inevitably attracted the Dutch. Still, the government in exile only reluctantly let itself be pulled in that direction. When General MacArthur reached the outskirts of the Dutch East Indies much earlier than Admiral Mountbatten, the Royal Netherlands Navy was irritated by the British refusal to let Dutch warships join the Americans. Still, even then they hoped that Mountbatten would be first in the Dutch East Indies, if only to keep out the Australians fighting under MacArthur. In all colonial matters it was thought that the British could be trusted, but it was only prudent not to take any chances with the Australians. Ironically MacArthur was trying to persuade the Dutch by dropping hints that once the British had reconquered part of the Dutch East Indies, it would be difficult to get rid of them afterwards.[18] In this rather tense atmosphere in the summer of 1945 the transfer of the greater part of MacArthur's command area to Mountbatten was received by the Dutch with mixed feelings. The 'Oboe' plans of the American General had been taken seriously by the Dutch, while the British had only just reached Rangoon. Politically, the transfer was welcome. Militarily, however, it was certain by now that the British were the slower of the two allies.[19] Yet they were now ordered to reconquer the whole of the Dutch East Indies. This meant that the return of the Dutch would take much more time than expected. Fearing that the Japanese would use this respite to arm the Indonesian population, the Dutch were in a hurry. Not surprisingly, irritation with Mountbatten's plans grew as they compared them with the quick results that MacArthur had promised. Leaving aside the point that this general had seriously underestimated the strength of the Japanese on Java, the Dutch feared that the British would first concentrate on Malaya and Singapore. The Dutch East Indies would be left alone till these British interests were secured. For once, the Dutch fretted at the links binding them to the British. The transport situation made things even worse. With the

Netherlands now liberated, Dutch conscripts and volunteers became available for shipment to the Far East. Arguing that British veterans were a sounder military investment than Dutch recruits, the allies refused to free Dutch troopships from allied shipping pools. This meant that Anglo-Dutch co-operation during the Second World War ended on a rather sour note.[20] Worse was to come.

During the first post-war years Anglo-Dutch co-operation developed along two lines — one in Europe, the other in the Far East. As to the first, the two countries and their armed forces worked harmoniously together. The Royal Netherlands Navy, for instance, asked for and obtained a British flag officer on loan to assist with the modernisation of the fleet and the digestion of lessons learned during the war.[21] The Naval Staff College in the Hague was restructured with help from the Royal Navy, and the British Admiralty expressed its willingness to plan for joint exercises, the exchange of officers, the use of each other's naval bases and dockyards, standardisation of equipment, pooling of naval intelligence, and so on. Moreover, since 1943 the Royal Netherlands Navy had been making plans for a completely new fleet comprising several task forces. To form the nucleus of this fleet a light aircraft-carrier was taken over from the Royal Navy.[22]

In the Far East, Anglo-Dutch politico-military relations developed along very different lines. The unexpectedly swift surrender of Japan created a vacuum of power in the Dutch East Indies that could not be filled by British or Dutch forces at once. The Indonesian nationalists now came to the fore, weeks before the first British and British-Indian troops landed on Java. Reluctant to use Asian soldiers against Indonesian nationalists, Admiral Mountbatten decided to negotiate with Sukarno. In choosing this line he was also influenced by his recent Burmese experiences. In that country a native politician who had collaborated with the Japanese had had to be accepted. That arrangement had worked reasonably well, and with many Dutch internees and allied prisoners of war kept as hostages by the Indonesian nationalists, Mountbatten saw no alternative but to apply this Burmese policy to the Dutch East Indies.[23] Not surprisingly, the Dutch were extremely frustrated by this decision, the more so as they were at first refused entrance to Java. Only after a considerable delay were Dutch troops allowed to disembark, while the structure of the British command was kept operative till November 1946. This meant that the Dutch were not allowed to act according to their own views. They were even forced, under British supervision, to accept a cease-fire and to work out a political arrangement with their opponents. It was only after the British had left that a full-scale military operation against the Indonesian Republic became a serious option for the Dutch. In the meantime they fretted at the British reins, first and foremost the Commander-in-Chief of the Royal Netherlands Navy. During these years he nourished a marked anti-British sentiment, suspecting the darkest motives behind British actions and even expecting a British takeover in the Dutch East Indies as soon as the Dutch had been forced into the background.[24] This suspicion soon faded away, but irritations persisted. The Indonesian nationalists, for instance, bought weapons and other military equipment abroad with money that had been earned by the export of all kinds of goods that had been found on Dutch-owned plantations and in Dutch-owned mines. Both import and export were of course forbidden by the Dutch, but were kept up through large-scale smuggling. British companies, and even minor British officials in Singapore and in Malaya were suspected of profiting from this business.[25] Again, the Royal Netherlands Navy took a rather strong anti-British position. Its Commander-in-Chief in the Far East, expecting to be detailed to command the whole of the Royal Netherlands Navy, even went as far as to doubt his ability to function properly in the Hague. There he would not be able to avoid working closely with officers of the Royal Navy. He foretold that his anti-British feelings would prevent him from accepting them as allies.[26]

In Europe, however, this attitude was unacceptable. There were so many ties between the two countries and their armed forces that the Far Eastern troubles could not break these ties. It was clear that the growing fear of the Soviet Union strengthened these ties even more. In case of a Soviet attack on Western Europe, the Royal Netherlands Navy simply planned to cross the North Sea once again and seek refuge in British harbours. That is why she retained 25 per cent of the crew on warships temporarily out of duty.[27] In the Far East too, the deterrent effect of communism brought the Dutch closer to the British. Rumours about an alliance in which Singapore, Malaya, Australia and New Zealand would participate were picked up in Batavia, and immediately the Dutch indicated that they hoped to be asked to join the club. That would not only enhance the security of the East Indies, it would offer the Dutch an argument for prolonging their stay in the Far East.[28] This Dutch eagerness to join an alliance in which Great Britain took part was not, however, fully unreserved. Again it was the Royal Netherlands Navy that expressed these reservations. Their main problem was uncertainty about how to defend themselves against the communist threat.[29] At sea, a Western alliance looked overwhelmingly strong at that time. On the Continent, however, the Red Armies cast a long shadow. Consequently, there was no lack of people who wanted the West to invest primarily in land and air power. According to their views, sea power should be left to the British and Americans. Together these two nations were strong enough to cope without additional naval forces.

In the Netherlands this strategic debate was soon the topic of conversation. Of course, the Royal Netherlands Navy warned against an exclusive continental commitment. To defend the importance of sea power and ample naval forces they pointed out the lessons of two World Wars. Their opponents were not impressed. What they questioned was not the relevance of sea power for a western alliance. The question was which nations should take care of that strategic factor. It was argued that Great Britain and the United States were better equipped and located than the Netherlands to keep the seas safe for the alliance. Soon these arguments were echoed in the English-speaking countries and once again the Royal Netherlands Navy felt threatened by her bigger sisters.

As regards Great Britain and the Royal Navy, the same forces that seemed to have obstructed the Dutch in the Dutch East Indies, now wanted to drive the Dutch, their age-old naval and colonial competitors, into a purely continental corner. All this, moreover, had happened before. To explain the game the British were playing, it was pointed out that the Netherlands had not lost its dominant naval and maritime position by opposing the British. The decline only set in when the Dutch Republic had been allied to Great Britain against a dominant continental power. Against Bourbon France the Dutch had acquiesced in 'task specialisation', giving priority to their army, and leaving dominance at sea to Great Britain.

Another anti-British argument came from more recent experience: the Second World War. That conflict had taught the Dutch that to buy influence in an alliance, ample military and maritime resources were needed. Without ships, planes and men, a government in exile does not carry weight among powerful allies, while purely national goals could not be looked after during a coalition war. For instance, as long as national military and maritime assets were integrated in alliance pools, they were effectively out of reach of a government in exile. This sometimes bitter and humiliating experience led to two conclusions.

Firstly, on a national level, the armed forces should be harmoniously structured in order to avoid any unnecessary dependence on allies. Secondly, the complete integration of all armed forces in an alliance system should be avoided. These arguments were enforced by the Royal Netherlands Navy. They clearly felt threatened at that time by the prospect of entering an alliance of which the Royal Navy (and the US Navy) formed prominent parts. Gradually, however, these fears abated, as the dreaded scenario did not materialise. Co-operation with Great Britain, already close during the preceding years, flourished, unspoiled now by Far Eastern troubles or suspicions as to the country's proper contribution to NATO. Just as the British clashed with the Americans over Suez, the Netherlands had to accept American intervention in their New Guinea confrontation with Indonesia. Between themselves however, it seemed as if Great Britain's relative decline brought the British and Dutch closer together.

Once in NATO, the aforementioned fears of the Royal Netherlands Navy evaporated. With the exception of their New Guinea commitment, the Netherlands could now concentrate on the western hemisphere, and this meant, especially for the navy, a co-operation with the British that grew closer every year. (As to the Netherlands army, co-operation with its British counterpart stopped to a large extent in the early 1950s, when it adapted to the American organisation structure). When new weapons systems were developed, the Dutch turned almost automatically to the British for information. And even when the British themselves became dependent on the United States, the Dutch tried to get what they wanted from the British, before seriously approaching the Americans. The nuclear submarine is a case in point.[30] By the end of the 1950s the Royal Netherlands Navy was considering the step to nuclear propulsion for its submarines. National research and industrial activities were started, but mainly with an eye to take matters up with the British. Realising that the United States was leading the field, the Royal Netherlands Navy was not opposed to shortcuts. Being more familiar with the British, it first tried to obtain what it needed through the Royal Navy. Only when it was told that the British could not comply without a bilateral Dutch–American agreement, did the Royal Netherlands Navy approach the United States. Although this British attitude was reasonable, it rankled with the Dutch. They felt themselves excluded from a special relationship and complained that they got only the crumbs from a rich table. Their own special relationship with the British certainly had its advantages. Yet the Dutch sometimes felt that a more NATO-integrated or West-European Union approach would offer more options and greater flexibility.[31] This line, however, was not followed very consistently. For instance, when confronted at the end of the 1950s with evidence that research co-operation between Great Britain, France and the Federal Republic of Germany was running into difficulties, the Dutch Minister of Defence immediately told the Admiralty Board of the Royal Netherlands Navy that this was a golden opportunity to strengthen the relations with the British.[32]

At about the same time the Royal Navy was trying to make NATO's Channel Command into an exclusive British affair. The French, at that time still full members of the alliance, should have protested, but tried to barter their influence in Channel Command for a more prominent position in the Iberian Atlantic Area. This left the Royal Netherlands Navy with no other option than to oppose the British. After some pressure, the latter showed willingness to listen to allied advice.[33] Also promising was a British offer to collaborate on a new post-Leander frigate design. The Dutch reaction was favourable, provided the project involved a more equal distribution among British and Dutch industries. However, the Dutch Board of Admiralty soon doubted British sincerity in this respect. Still, this Board was not without hope of changing the attitude of the British. Anyway, its policy was to use this project in such a way that 'in the future co-operation between the two navies becomes a necessity'.[34]

Shortly after this optimistic note, the new frigate programme ran into difficulties. Complaints about British preference for one-sided business deals could be heard more frequently now in Dutch naval circles. In 1967, for instance, the Netherlands placed an order for military and naval equipment worth 16 million guilders in Great Britain. The other way round just under 4 million had been spent.

What made matters worse was the conviction of the Dutch that in many respects their war industry was qualitatively superior to the British. The Dutch Flag-Officer Materiel naturally deplored this unequal relationship. To turn to other countries was impossible, however, at least as long as the Navy valued its operational and logistical ties to its British sister. However, well aware of the pressure from Dutch war industries to opt for a less exclusively British orientation, he stated that in time the importance of the Royal Navy would decline to such an extent that the Dutch would be pardoned for looking for other partners. In his opinion the British were so far unsurpassed in ship designing and mechanical engineering, and in the development of naval tactics. In other respects, he thought that the Royal Netherlands Navy had little to learn from the British and little to gain by buying British.[35]

In the end, the frigate programme could not be carried through. From this experience the Dutch Chief of the Naval Staff came to the conclusion that such ambitious projects needed longer preparation time and more high-level coaching.[36] This certainly did not make him change course. On the contrary, what he had in mind was to make sure that such a failure would not happen a second time. The principle of co-operation was not questioned, certainly not now, as the marines of the two countries had already moved one step farther in the direction of integration.[37] The decision of the Netherlands government to give up the western half of New Guinea left the Royal Netherlands Marine Corps without a major assignment. Almost simultaneously, roughly the same misfortune struck its British counterpart, when Great Britain retreated from East of Suez.

With characteristic flexibility, the two organisations recovered from this shock by adopting a more NATO-oriented profile. Pressed by the United States, the strategy of the western alliance changed from mass retaliation to flexible response in the course of the 1960s. Crisis management became an essential part of the new NATO strategy and the British and Dutch marines formed sharp-edged instruments for its implementation. The growing imbalance of military power between the alliance and the Soviet Union at NATO's northern flank became the final reason for integrating the marines of the two countries. The UK/NL amphibious force was the result of all these considerations. In its wake, the Royal Netherlands Navy and the Royal Navy are now projecting more and more power in the Norwegian Sea. The Royal Air Force is perhaps following suit.[38] No doubt the co-operation between British and Dutch armed forces will be further stimulated by these developments.

The dominant role played by Great Britain in Dutch foreign policy for such a long time has been taken over by the United States in many respects. The special relationship between Washington and London has both obscured and softened the importance of this change. Only now, when the influence of the United States is no longer as far-reaching as it used to be, do the Dutch seem to realise that a new era is dawning. For the first time in centuries the naturalness of an English/American connection is questioned in some quarters. The foreign policy of the Netherlands was founded on the opinion that the English-speaking nations could never be strong enough. Their relative decline shakes the very foundation on which the Dutch international position is built. A purely European security system has no attraction for the Netherlands. Such a system could easily be dominated by a Franco-German combination. Notwithstanding its many economic ties to the Federal Republic, the Netherlands is very interested in balancing this dependence with bonds to the English-speaking world.

Traditionally Anglo-Dutch co-operation has centred around maritime interests and a balance of power in Europe. Now that America is losing some of its strength, the possibility that the attention of Great Britain and the Netherlands may turn in an easterly direction cannot be dismissed. In both countries proposals have been put forward to structure the armed forces so as to conform to a continental bias.[39] In my opinion, both countries should be extremely wary of following this path. Both know from previous experience that balancing a continental commitment to a maritime orientation is essential to their long-term security and well-being. It is precisely because a European security system might become a reality in the near future that the Netherlands and Great Britain should keep this balance in mind. If they fail in this respect it would mean a loss to the whole of Europe.

NOTES

1. G. Teitler, 'De Slagluchtmacht'. *Mededelingen van de sectie Militaire Geschiedenis Landmachtstaf 7* (1984), pp. 93–146.
2. This title is taken from N. Tarling, '"A Vital British Interest": Britain, Japan, and the Security of Netherlands-India in the Interwar Period'. *Journal of Southeast-Asian Studies* 12:2 (1978), pp. 180–218, 207.
3. All correspondence by the naval attaché, Lieutenant-Commander A. de Booy, is in the Algemeen Rijksarchief, The Hague (ARA): Archief Marinestaf 1886–1940. See his letters to the Chief of Naval Staff of 6 June, 30 and 31 July and 21 October 1936, 18 January and 18 August 1937.
4. Tarling, Vital British Interest, pp. 209–11.
5. *Ibid.*, p. 182.
6. This letter by Captain A. Sluys, dated 1 March 1922, is in the De Booy papers in the Archief Marinestaf.
7. Tarling *op. cit.*, pp. 208–14. See also A. Shai, *Origins of the War in the East. Britain, China and Japan 1937–39* (London, 1976), and P. Lowe, *Great Britain and the Origins of the Pacific War. A Study of British Policy in East Asia 1937–1941* (Oxford, 1977).
8. De Booy to the Chief of Naval Staff, 30 July 1936.
9. *Ibid.*, 6 June 1936.

10. See, for these developments, ARA: Archief Koloniën, 1 May 1937 L 10, 4 June 1937 K 13, 23 August 1937 S 21, 11 August 1937 C 20, 12 October 1937 L 26, 11 January 1938 L 1, 6 October 1939 U 41, 11 October 1939 J 42.

11. De Booy to the Chief of Naval Staff, 1 and 26 January and 20 September 1937.

12. Ph. M. Bosscher, *De Koninklijke Marine in de Tweede Wereldoorlog*, 3 vols (Franeker, 1984–1989), I, chapters 7, 9.

13. M. Matloff and E. M. Snell, *Strategic Planning for Coalition Warfare 1941–1942* (Washington, D.C., 1953).

14. For the Singapore conferences, see Bosscher, *De Koninklijke Marine in de Tweede Wereldoorlog I*, pp. 71–83.

15. G. Teitler, 'Strategic Planning in Exile, 1942–1945: "Germany First" and the Future of the Netherlands in Europe and Asia', *Marineblad* 99 (1989), pp. 58–64.

16. Chr. Thorne, *Allies of a Kind. The United States, Britain and the War against Japan, 1941–1945* (London, 1978), chapters 6, 7, 8.

17. C. E. L. Helfrich, *Mémoires*, 2 vols (Amsterdam, 1950).

18. Thorne, *Allies of a Kind*, chapters 20, 22. Detailed information can be found in the papers of H. J. van Mook in ARA, and of Admirals C. E. L. Helfrich and J. Th. Furstner in Afdeling Maritieme Historie van de Marinestaf (Historical Department of the Netherlands Naval Staff, The Hague, AMH).

19. D. Clayton James, *The Years of MacArthur II* (Boston, 1975), chapter 17; Thorne, *Allies of a Kind*, chapter 27.

20. ARA: Ministerie voor Algemene Oorlogvoering van het Koninkrijk (AOK), Box 110, file 'Oorlog met Japan 1945'.

21. Admiral Furstner to the First Sea Lord, 7 August 1947 [AMH: Persoonlijk Archief Furstner].

22. *Ibid.*, memorandum by the First Sea Lord: 'Postwar Relations between the Royal Navy and the Allied Navies'.

23. See, for the first months after the Japanese surrender, J. Th. Bank, *Katholieken en de Indonesische Revolutie* (Baarn, 1983), Chapter 4.

24. G. Teitler, 'Een vergeten strijd. Patrouilles, smokkel, infiltratie', in G. Teitler and P. M. H. Groen, eds, *De Politionele Acties* (Amsterdam, 1987), pp. 144–60.

25. *Ibid.*

26. Vice-Admiral A. S. Pinke to the Commander-in-Chief Royal Netherlands Navy, Lieutenant-Admiral Helfrich, 22 May 1948. ARA, Archief Pinke 19.

27. Report of the meeting of Vice-Admiral A. S. Pinke with his staff, 9 July 1948. [ARA: Archief Marinestaf 1945–1948, S 16/4/8].

28. See AMH: Commissie voor Militaire aangelegenheden van de Ronde Tafel Conferentie (Commission for Military Affairs to the Round Table Conference between the Kingdom of the Netherlands, the Indonesian Republic and the Federal States of Indonesia), meetings of 6 September, 1 and 4 October 1949.

29. See, for the following section, G. Teitler, *Enige aspecten van het maritiem-strategisch denken in Nederland* (Den Helder, 1980).
30. Teitler, 'Een Nederlandse Nautilus', *Marineblad* 98 (1988), pp. 410–18.
31. CAD: Archief staatssecretaris van Marine (ASM) 633, 'Rapport van de bespreking te Londen op 18 november 1957 van minister Staf met zijn Britse ambtgenoot'.
32. AMH: notulen Admiraliteitsraad (AR) 14 January 1958.
33. *Ibid.*, 5 May 1959 and 30 October 1962.
34. *Ibid.*, 25 July and 8 August 1967, 26 March and 20 August 1968. See, for the quotation, AR 22 April 1969.
35. See, for this conclusion, CAD: ASM 160, several letters by the Flag-officer Materiel, Rear-Admiral J. Doorenbos, to the Under-secretary of Defence for the Navy in the Autumn of 1968 and in the first months of 1969.
36. CAD: ASM 160, reply of the Chief of Naval Staff to the Flag-officer Materiel, 25 August 1969.
37. H. Mallant, 'Het Korps Mariniers en de Noordflank', in G. Teitler and C. Homan, eds, *Het Korps Mariniers 1942–heden* (Amsterdam, 1985), pp. 67–75.
38. See the articles in the special 'De Noordflank en de NAVO', *Marineblad*, 97 (1986), pp. 595–677.
39. P. M. Volten, *Voor het zelfde geld meer defensie* (The Hague, 1987) and J. Baylis, ed., *Alternative Approaches to British Defence Policy* (London, 1983).

6

A NECESSARY EVIL.
THE ARMED FORCES AND SOCIETY IN
THE NETHERLANDS

J. C. H. Blom

The Dutch past harbours a treasure of impressive and glorious military occurrences.[1] The most famous of these were achieved — and this congress with 'Anglo-Dutch Partnership' in its title is a good opportunity to recall this — in the seventeenth century naval wars against England. One might even consider the Four Days' Battle in 1666 and the expedition to Chatham in 1667 as the highlights of Dutch glory at sea. But there has been much more. Very early in the fight against Philip II of Spain, a not unimportant naval battle was fought: the battle of the Zuiderzee in 1573. Later on in the Eighty Years' War, the battle of Downs was of great importance. In these few examples, only the control of the seas close to the Netherlands was at stake. Early in the seventeenth century the Dutch fleet also appeared elsewhere in the world; in the Mediterranean for example, where Heemskerck fell at Gibraltar in 1607 and Michiel de Ruyter at Sicily in 1676, and in the Baltic, where the Dutch fleet restored order more than once. In the East and West Indies it was mainly armed merchantmen which were active, but here as well there was occasion for marked military action, especially in the West. And, of course, the capture of the Spanish Silverfleet in 1628 should not be forgotten in this context. No wonder that the names of quite a few Dutch admirals are very well known and still live on in nursery rhymes and folk-songs. Although, according to the stereotyped pictures of the Netherlands as a seafaring country, military glory was chiefly gained at sea; in fact military activities on land were at least as important. One could easily defend the statement that the Dutch Revolt resulted in a Dutch State partly, and perhaps even mainly, because it gradually changed into the famous Eighty Years' War, which was largely waged on land. Obviously this war did not yield only successes (no more than did the naval battles). The first campaign of William of

84

Orange in 1568, for example, resulted in a complete failure, in spite of a small victory at Heiligerlee at the beginning of the campaign. But considering the Eighty Years' War as a whole, there certainly were some remarkable achievements. Both Stadholder Maurice and his cousin William Louis grew into internationally prominent strategists and army reformers.

Next to various battles (the battle of Nieuwpoort in 1600 is, partly because of the nice round figure, indelibly printed on the minds of the Dutch), it was mainly sieges which were of importance. At first, only the defence of the cities against Spanish troops was at stake, and from time to time the townspeople played a remarkable role alongside the garrisons (as was the case in Haarlem in 1573 and in Leiden in 1574). But later on, offensive sieges became more important. At the end of the sixteenth century Maurice closed 'The Fence of the Seven Provinces', as it was called. His brother and successor, Frederick Henry, managed to enlarge the territory south of the Great Rivers: the conquest of 's-Hertogenbosch, 1629, is undoubtedly his most famous feat of arms. As a direct result of this he received the nickname of 'De Stedendwinger', which roughly corresponds to the English 'The Conqueror of Cities'.

Although the great successes were achieved in the seventeenth century, as one would expect from the strength of the Dutch Republic in that period, it would be wrong not to mention the two following periods. First, it is the early nineteenth century which draws one's attention. In 1812, Dutch pontoneers played a heroic part in the retreat of Napoleon's army at the Berezina in Russia. And later, in 1815, the actions of the Dutch troops under the command of the Prince of Orange at Quatre Bras, preceding the battle of Waterloo, were also of some importance. The Belgian Rebellion of 1830 also led to military activities, both in that year and in 1831, which drew much attention. The actions of Van Speyk and the Ten Days' Campaign gave rise to much enthusiasm. Secondly, the armed forces were able to distinguish themselves to some extent in the five days' battle against Germany in May 1940, which ended in disaster, and in the allied war against that country, in which the Royal Netherlands Navy and the Irenebrigade participated.

Colonial history gives us many more examples. Many, often successful, but at times also catastrophic, expeditions had to be undertaken in the nineteenth century to establish Dutch rule in the colonies. The Aceh wars especially cost a lot, but yielded much military honour as well. In the twentieth century, Japan gradually became the major enemy in the Pacific. During the war against that country, which was waged in alliance, an important part was played by the then very young Dutch Air Force for the first time. From this period, the battle of the Java Sea, in which Karel Doorman played such a heroic part, is also very well known in the Netherlands. And after the Second World War, probably the most extensive Dutch military action of all time took place. After the Japanese occupation, Dutch activities in the Dutch East Indies, which were meant to restore order and authority, resulted in a war against the native nationalist movement. This conflict, mainly a guerilla war, with restrictions on the Dutch side of a policy which prevented uninhibited action, was lost mainly because it *was* a guerilla war. As soon as more traditional and ambitious military actions were undertaken, the Dutch armed forces were able to boast of great successes.

This small selection from a vast number of Dutch military activities makes it clear that there is ample material for a strong military tradition, for a prominent place for the armed forces in Dutch society and for a nationalistic and also a triumphalist look at our own past. There are indeed many examples of such historiography. Next to the older and more specialised military historiography, one can also find such passages in the works of the most prominent historians of the nineteenth and twentieth centuries. I will restrict myself to two examples taken from the great work of P. J. Blok, which was first published in eight volumes around 1900: *Geschiedenis van het Nederlandse volk* (History of the Dutch People). Blok concludes his summarised opinion of Stadholder Maurice, which is certainly not positive in all respects, by saying that 'posterity' also honours him as 'the great warrior, the excellent mathematician, the brilliant creator of an army which became in his hands and in those of his brother, an excellent tool through which the liberty of the state of the Netherlands, primarily a creation of their father, was forever ensured'.[2] About the end of the Four Days' Battle, Blok wrote (I avoid the question of the correctness of his opinions from the modern point of view):

> The main body of the Dutch armed forces was but for a moment in danger, for at the crucial moment De Ruyter hoisted the red flag as a sign for the general attack. The English lines broke in various places and presently the Dutch were chasing the enemy fleet. The entire English fleet would have been destroyed had not a thick fog prevented pursuit. Thus, this battle ended in victory and the states' navy, though badly damaged, sailed into the Wielingen decked with flags and pennants, triumphantly towing six English ships, 300 prisoners, Ayscue and the body of his colleague Berkeley; evidence

of a victory which should have silenced all English assertions and shouts of joy about an English victory.[3]

Until a few decades ago, many Dutch children learned about their nation's military activities in words like these through school-books and boys' books.

However, such passages are not the most characteristic ones in Dutch historiography. There was, and still is, hardly any question of a strong military tradition deeply rooted in society, or of a prominent place for the armed forces therein. Where national complacency was at stake, attention was mainly concentrated on religious strife, commercial achievements, the arts and from time to time on science and burning political issues. Far from being militaristic, Dutch society has often been characterised as bourgeois. In 1941, A. J. C. Rüter mentioned the 'spirit of liberty and tolerance, realism and being bourgeois' as the most characteristic qualities of the Dutch nation.[4] As a complement to this widely-held view C. M. Schulten stated: 'The people of the Netherlands were never militaristic in the past. Nor was the majority even anti-militaristic on principle. The people of the Netherlands were for the greater part non-militaristic. They were a nation of civilians, who accepted they needed an army, but did not love it'.[5] From this point of view, military heroism was of secondary importance.

In this chapter, the background of this attitude and its consequences for the relations between the armed forces and society, especially during the twentieth century, are the main issue. Why is it that, in spite of the fact that military events played such an important part in the birth and early prosperity of the Dutch state, the military element in Dutch society has always been of minor importance? The differences between the Netherlands and countries such as Britain, France and Germany in this respect are obvious. What were the consequences of this state of affairs for the armed forces, especially in relation to society as a whole? It will be clear that all these questions cannot be dealt with exhaustively in the available space. Besides, the problem has hardly ever been studied extensively. It is not possible to refer back to some series of penetrating monographs.[6] Therefore my answers will be highly subjective and often not more than stray remarks about certain aspects of the issue. First, however, I should point out that there is some danger of exaggeration. Sometimes the terms being used are too strong. It is very often a matter of accent, of more or less, of degree, and not of a complete absence of interest or appreciation of the military aspects in

Dutch society. The necessity for a military force, for example, has never been seriously questioned, although some anxious observers have suggested otherwise. This was never the case even during those periods in the nineteenth and twentieth centuries, in the heyday of anti-militaristic, pacifist and unilateral disarmament movements; nor did all these movements strive after the complete abolition of the armed forces. Those political parties who believed that there should be a military force have always been in the majority and have dominated the various cabinets. Therefore, those who wish to discuss the quality of the armed forces should not start by looking at the opposition, but at the dominating majority. In this context it is also interesting to note that the anti-armament movements scored their greatest successes in their fight against very specific and concrete aspects of the armed forces and defence policy: the Naval Act in the 1920s and nuclear armament in the 1970s and 1980s. However, even if they did manage to mobilise impressive masses of people for their aims (by means of demonstrations and petitions), it hardly changed the way in which the Dutch people cast their vote.[7] Besides, movements like the ones just mentioned were often opposed by counter-organisations, though these had a smaller, or rather less manifest, following. Just think of organisations such as *Ons leger* (Our Army) and *Onze vloot* (the Navy League) and committees like the ones against unilateral disarmament and 'against undermining the defences of our country' in the 1920s and 1930s, and more recently the *Interkerkelijk Comité voor Tweezijdige Ontwapening* (Interdenominational Committee for Bilateral Disarmament), the antipode of the *Interkerkelijk Vredesberaad* (Interdenominational Peace Movement).

The complaints about the lack of popularity and prestige of a career in the armed forces have also been exaggerated at times. But wasn't it a fact that people with an army career were often given the cold shoulder and sometimes even called murderers? And wasn't it a fact that the armed forces were considered 'the dregs of society'? Was it possible to recruit enough talented people for training at one of the officers' training schools? It is my impression that things were not in such a bad way as was sometimes believed. Of course there have been fluctuations in the popularity of the armed forces, or of a career within that institution, and it is true that they lacked the prestige they had in Britain, France or Germany for example. But ever since the prestige of a military career began to be measured more seriously, which was after the Second World War, the results were certainly not shocking or alarming. So-called 'professional prestige stratifications', which were drafted in 1953 and 1982, showed that the commanding officer (i.e., Colonel) ended up somewhere near the parson and the secondary schoolteacher, and the non-commissioned officer close to the policeman and the self-employed farmer. Soldiers and sailors were not included in the scales. So even if the higher officers did not come anywhere near the professions such as professor, doctor, judge, notary or mayor of a big city, they did belong to the highest social strata.[8] In surveys like these, however, it may be necessary to think relatively. An assessment of the average opinions of the entire population was undertaken. In certain circles, however, opinions could be very different. Among a section of the nobility and aristocracy, for instance, there was a clear tradition of 'becoming an officer'. And the absence of the ordinary soldier and sailor from the scales calls attention to the fact that those ranks have almost disappeared as a profession. Once, in the nineteenth century and earlier, they did indeed belong to the lowest strata of society everywhere in Europe. So this was not a situation which was specifically Dutch. And the attitude towards compulsory military service should not be linked to the prestige of a military career: the 'balen' of conscripts ('balen' is a Dutch word which expresses how much most conscripts detested having to serve) and their aversion to entering the army are comparatively normal phenomena, which are not in any way alarming for the armed forces.

The navy was generally more attractive than the army or air force, which is in line with the maritime tradition, so important in the Netherlands, especially in relation to commerce and colonialism. On the other hand, the air force, with its atmosphere of advanced technology and adventure is nowadays more attractive to certain groups of the new generation. Another element of appeal and prestige for the armed forces as a whole may also be their special ties with the House of Orange. These ties, which were never absent even in the days of the Republic, were, as Amersfoort shows us, especially cherished during the nineteenth century, when the process of conscious nation-building was in full swing.[9] This situation was still much the same in the twentieth century. It is well known how much Queen Wilhelmina felt these ties. It is therefore no coincidence that numerous public ceremonies attended by our armed forces are those at which members of the Royal Household are also present, such as inaugurations, the ceremonies connected with the opening of the States-General, the reception of heads of state, and so on.

That it would be incorrect to describe the attitude of the Dutch people towards their armed forces in too negative terms can be illustrated by drawing attention to the final debate over the abolition in 1898 of the 'remplacantenregeling', a system which made it possible to pay someone else to complete your terms of national service for you.[10] This debate should be seen against the background of a much wider debate on defence and the armed forces in general, which had been carried on since it became evident in 1866 and 1870 that under the existing system the security of the Netherlands was only very marginally guaranteed.[11] Returning to Parliament in 1898, when the decision was made to abolish the above system of replacement, we may observe that none of the speakers took a negative view on defence or the armed forces in general, irrespective of whether they were for or against the system. The odd note from socialist quarters or some confessional apprehension about moral standards in the barracks did not shatter this general positive attitude. Almost all those present were interested only in how to strengthen Dutch defences and improve the armed forces. The supporters of abolition of the system, who finally decided the matter in their favour, had some very positive arguments at hand for their point of view: under the new system the social and intellectual élite would also be compelled to participate in the armed forces; it would be in the interest of social justice; and everybody would realise how valuable and important the tasks of the armed forces actually were. The then Minister of Home Affairs, H. Goeman Borgesius, put it like this: 'Then, all ranks will be represented in the barracks; no soldier will be banished from respectable circles just because he is a soldier; serving will be considered an honour instead of a shame'.[12]

For that matter, my warning against exaggeration does not affect the correctness of my initial statement: In the Netherlands, military traditions are relatively weak and the role of the armed forces and the military in Dutch public life is of secondary importance. It is not difficult to discover those aspects of Dutch history which have combined to create a situation like this. The Dutch Republic originated from a rebellion against a centralising monarchy. This was one of the reasons why this state, which was in many respects a strange phenomenon in Europe, did not have a strong centre in the form of a royal court in which both nobility and military took up important positions. The States-General in the Hague did not act as a powerful centralising authority either. In fact there were a great many larger and smaller centres of authority. The most important of these were, in changing mutual relations, the court of the stadholder, the States of Holland and the mayors of Amsterdam. But they always had to reckon with the influence of the other provinces, cities and ranks. This division into numerous small entities was also obvious in the formal federal political structure of the Republic, to which was linked an equally divided financial structure. That was also the reason why both the army and the navy, whose higher ranks were often very much inclined towards the court of the stadholder, could not develop into powerful bases of authority or into important sources of centralised power. They were always dependent on their many masters for money.

Whereas the influence of the nobility was comparatively small in the Republic (once again, there is some danger of exaggeration), the influence of the bourgeoisie was very strong. That is why, in politics, the financial and commercial interests of the urban bourgeoisie were predominant, leaving very little room for military–strategic interests or for arguments in favour of military honour and glory. It was certainly possible that commercial interests might lead to military action, but on the whole the wish for peace dominated, as peace was considered more favourable for trade than war. The tendency to pursue a policy of territorial expansion was therefore very small. J. C. Boogman made a well-known and illuminating distinction between a dominating maritime–commercial tradition in foreign policy on the one hand and a continental–expansive tradition on the other, which was of secondary importance most of the time.[13] This general domination of the maritime–commercial tradition resulted in a certain aloofness towards territorial expansion in Europe. The urge for expansion was mainly aimed at widening commercial interests both within and outside Europe. If necessary, this could result in wresting freedom of trade or in establishing trading posts in the colonies, but territorial expansion was seldom or never an aim in itself. Therefore the readiness to spend money on the armed forces without there being any question of direct and tangible results was not very great. As a result, the position of the armed forces remained of secondary importance.

In Europe, and especially during the seventeenth century, the Republic played a very prominent role, which was mainly based on its remarkable economic prosperity. But as the other European Powers made up their arrears, the Republic found it more and more difficult to bear the financial burden of this prominent place. And the (sometimes very extensive) military activities (direct or indirect through support to allies) were a part of that burden. These financial problems strengthened the tendency of the Dutch Republic to prefer peace and neutrality to active participation in the political and military conflicts in Europe. In the eighteenth century it was impossible for the Republic to avoid becoming internationally involved altogether, but its heart was not in it. This had its effects on the armed forces. By the end of the eighteenth century, the problem of neglect of both the army and the navy had become urgent. During the nineteenth century, the conclusion that the Netherlands was only a small European state had become inevitable. After the turbulent periods of the Batavian Republic and the years of French rule, the Netherlands became a more centralised national monarchy. Its first king, William I, did try to turn this state into at least a medium-sized power, with a large colonial realm, but his efforts can only be seen as a temporary domination of the continental–expansive tradition. Inherent in this was a prominent place in society for the armed forces to which the king attached great value. The failure of his efforts resulted in a definite recognition of the Netherlands, by this time a parliamentary–constitutional monarchy, as a small state. From then on neutrality in international conflicts was considered essential for the protection of commercial interests and the colonies. Under the influence of legalistic traditions in international law, and ethical motives, which had become very important in this century, foreign policy was getting more and more pacifist. This meant in practice that the Netherlands completely refrained from military initiatives, especially outside the colonies. Naturally, the defence of the national frontiers still remained the responsibility of the armed forces. But it was also assumed, implicitly and often also explicitly, that in the long run the survival of the Netherlands as an independent state would only be safe if the country could count on support against an eventual aggressor. And since it was supposed to be in the interest of the whole of Europe that the Netherlands should remain an independent state (after all, it would be in the interest of each of the Great Powers not to allow the Netherlands to fall into the hands of their rivals) the state could be sure of that support; neutrality would be rewarded. In this perception, a lengthy independent defence of the Netherlands was, if not impossible, then impossibly expensive. Besides, ever since the middle of this century, the various Liberal and Liberal–Conservative cabinets had pursued a very economical financial policy, partly in reaction to the financial policy of William I. It is not surprising that military expenses were continuously under pressure in a state which was still dominated by the commercially-minded middle classes. It is understandable that the armed forces were not much inspired by the role they were allotted.

Against the background of the developments which I have sketched, the position of the armed forces in the Netherlands in the second half of the nineteenth century is quite logical. They were a relatively weak military force with not much prestige in society, in spite of quite a bit of military glory in the past. For the men it was the same as anywhere else in Europe, namely, that the armed forces were 'the dregs of society'. And for the élite too, not much credit could be gained by it. The Netherlands were even less inclined than previously to look to power or military show to prove their excellence. W. J. Hofdijk expressed it beautifully in his historical works *Ons Voorgeslacht* (Our Ancestors), which was published in six volumes between 1860 and 1880. He concluded his work by triumphantly recalling that once upon a time the Netherlands had a position of authority in Europe. That this was somewhat in the past was no reason for sadness. For, 'It is better to be the most moral rather than the most powerful nation in the world'.[14]

This, I repeat, does not mean that the right to exist or the necessity for the armed forces was ever widely doubted. But why, how much and at what price has always been under discussion. It was mainly after the mediocre achievements of 1870, when both mobilisation and the defence of the national frontiers during the Franco-Prussian war were pictures of despair, that the debate on how the condition of the armed forces could be improved was begun.[15] In the background, the rise of a new and strong Germany on the eastern frontier, and the developments in the colonies, were important factors. Pacifist, and sometimes even anti-militaristic movements exercised some influence, but were never a real threat to the armed forces, however clamorous they tended to be.

Thus, after the low of 1870, the armed forces made a far more favourable impression during the First World War. It had cost much discussion and quite a bit of money since 1870, but as a result of all kinds of measures — the system of fortifications, the inundation line and army reforms — the neutrality of the Netherlands seemed to be guaranteed and supported from a military point of view. This was favourable to the armed forces, though there certainly was some backsliding now and then, particularly in the first decade after the First World War. This was a result of the aversion to war caused by the horrors of that conflict and of the retrenchment policy which was deemed necessary. On the whole, however, in the twentieth century the armed forces believe themselves to be firmly rooted in the Dutch state and an essential part of Dutch society as a necessity, without ever being considered as one of the most prominent, most characteristic or most central of institutions. Especially after the Second World War, the position of the armed forces was strengthened by the decision to abandon the policy of remaining neutral at all costs and to adapt the defence of the Netherlands to the Atlantic Alliance. I will return to this question at the end of the chapter.

When we look more closely at the position of the armed forces in the Netherlands in the twentieth century — unfortunately the technical and tactical skills of the army have to be left aside — it is obvious that the discussion in parliament about defence and the armed forces deserves some attention. When we attempt an overall survey of these discussions for the twentieth century, then it is apparent that some debates are intermingled, primarily the debate about the necessity for national defence — and thus the national armament. This question was discussed hotly and sometimes very emotionally, especially after the First World War and well into the thirties. It attracted much attention, but without saying that it was unimportant or that it had no influence on the position of the armed forces, I think that the significance of this debate can easily be overestimated. As previously observed, even in the heyday of anti-military, pacifist or unilateral disarmament movements, one-third of the members of parliament at most held views of this sort.

This also means that a second debate, mostly started by military men inside or outside parliament, was partly based on a wrong principle. Time and again fear of interference with the right of the armed forces to exist is to be heard in the discussions. In 1910 the Minister of War said, 'Perhaps no other member of the government than the War Minister has to take so much trouble to win the people's confidence'.[16] The spirit of the nation, as was often remarked, seemed to be abhorrent of defence. For instance, this should be apparent from the fact that when, in 1939, conscripts who had a job could be replaced by unemployed persons, who could earn more than their unemployment benefit, less than 10 per cent were willing to do so.[17] And officers, who liked to see their job as a 'vocation' (for, weren't they willing to give their lives for their country?) did not detect much appreciation from society, with all the attendant dangers of demotivation and social isolation. However, anxious statements about this were usually not acted upon. Sometimes they evoked solemn declarations of appreciation. But except for the financial aspects, which I will discuss later, they were concerned with few concrete matters. I think the main concerns were expressions of dissatisfaction about the relatively insignificant position of the armed forces in Dutch society already described. The comparison with some larger countries must have been painful. It is understandable that regular soldiers had some difficulty living with this, but it does not mean that all their complaints in this vein are always right. Generally they are at least somewhat exaggerated.

The essence of the parliamentary debate has always been the financial aspect. This was also the most concrete and urgent political problem which demanded a prompt answer. Many other more practical or technical issues were often connected with these financial problems, while the more essential and fundamental questions either remained open or were not discussed, because the answers were in fact given long before. These principal questions were certainly not discussed at length in parliament year after year. The defence debates in a more limited sense were not always the best framework in which those underlying questions could be considered. After the decisions about personal compulsory military service and some related questions, at the beginning of the twentieth century for instance, it was established that henceforth the Netherlands would have a military force comprising a permanent, not too large professional core and reserve troops of conscripts who could be readily mobilised and called into the army at about 20 years of age. The real strategic questions were by their nature inappropriate for public discussion in parliament. And foreign policy, highly relevant of course for defence and for the armed forces, was a separate field of discussion. Apart from that, foreign policy was very stable — until 1940 one of neutrality and after the Second World War one of participation in western alliances.

With the exception of the very special periods of mobilisation and war (when financial inhibitions almost fell away), in the financial debates the options were, roughly speaking, more important than the wishes of the armed forces or the international situation. It seems to me that in this the Netherlands does not differ from most other countries — certainly not from the smaller ones. One of the best illustrations of this consideration is still a statement of H. Colijn, issued in the twenties. Colijn was a former officer in the Dutch colonial army and a former Minister of War, and he was certainly favourably disposed towards the armed forces and defence.

Nevertheless, he thought that, 'in these financial circumstances we must get used to the idea that defending our territory against foreign hostilities during a longer period will have to be taken out of our defence system'.[18] There was a generally accepted need to be as economical as possible. This remained a subject of constant concern, even in the second half of the 1930s, when, because of international tension, the defence expenditure was increased. One member of parliament for instance was even in these circumstances very insistent on a cut-back of expenditure, 'lest money will be spent otherwise than strictly necessary and the army needlessly be brought into discredit'.[19] An important problem for those who made a stand for higher defence expenditure has always been that, given the non-military tradition, defence may indeed be seen as a necessity, but, compared to other ends its popularity is not always great in the Netherlands. In its most demagogic form the argument is somewhat as follows: With the money that this single high-priced jet-fighter costs we could build a number of schools for handicapped children. In this way defence is always exposed to a continuous stream of urgent reasons to economise.

When we switch to the question: 'How much was actually spent on the armed forces?' (in a certain sense this reflects the attitude of society towards defence and the armed forces), we find ourselves faced with an extremely difficult question. One can neither indicate the exact level of the defence expenditure, nor the precise meaning of it. For example, the question whether it is much or not much can only be answered comparatively. For that purpose we also need exact figures of expenditure on other issues, and also of the expenditures of other countries. As far as I know these are not available over a long period of time, nor is there certainty about the actual level of military expenditure in the Netherlands. Once I made an attempt to give a more precise answer to this question for the 1920s and 1930s. I only partially succeeded in doing so, and not everyone supported my figures.[20] Therefore I will now restrict myself to a rather rough impression which is certainly not demonstrable. I think that, generally speaking, the Netherlands is rather economical with its defence expenditures, but, when we look at other governments and especially those of smaller countries, we certainly cannot say that there has been a notable financial negligence of defence.

This can be amplified for different periods. In the period from 1870 up to 1914, a lot of money was spent on defence in connection with its reorganisation; certainly when we consider it as part of the total government expenditure, which was then connected with fewer issues. Roughly speaking defence took 20 per cent of expenditure.[21] During the First World War the expenditure of course increased. For four years there were a great many conscripts in the services and for other matters also it was necessary to spend large sums of money. During the 20 years after the First World War the pressure for economisation was great, though the feeling with respect to defence changed strongly about the middle of the thirties. Expressed as percentages of government expenditure it fluctuates between well over 10 and just under 10, with peaks in 1938 and 1939. Undoubtedly, the rise starting in the middle of the thirties set in too late and was insufficient to bring the defence to the standard required by some critics, bearing in mind the defeat of May 1940. In my opinion however, the confrontation with the German army and air forces would not have led to substantially better results, even with very much higher expenditure at a considerably earlier date, without a completely different situation prevailing in the rest of Europe.

Quickly leaving this sort of speculation, it is easy to appreciate that from mobilisation in 1939 until the end of the forties, when the Dutch troops left Indonesia, defence expenditure was extremely high — so high in fact, that partly because of it the Netherlands nearly went bankrupt a few times. As for the years afterwards, it seems safe to note the following, mainly based on Siccama's opinions.[22]

- Defence expenditure, not adjusted for inflation, is increasing, but its part of the total government spending decreases.
- In real figures, that is to say corrected figures, the operating costs of both personnel and materiel are remarkably stable, while on the contrary investments (the purchase of new weapons) show a considerable fluctuation.

When we try to study expenditure comparatively then I incline to think that the Dutch contribution to NATO has not been remarkably high, but certainly not very low either. Particularly in fulfilling its obligations, the Netherlands has rather a good name. Even in the latest austerity policy of the government, the argument of NATO obligations plays an important role, though it is not always the deciding factor.

This parliamentary and political interference with defence and the armed forces, specifically expressed by the provision of money, is perhaps the most important aspect of the relation between society and the armed forces. But it is also interesting to consider whether there was (and if so, in what way) a reflection in the armed forces of the relations and social developments in society at large, and conversely if, and in what way, the armed forces influence society, for instance in politics. To consider the first issue, it is important to realise that the armed forces are an exceptional element in Dutch society, just as in other countries. They are a conglomeration of separate and even more or less isolated organisations with their own specific features. They

have a very strict internal hierarchy and discipline and a professional
ethos in which preparedness to die for the nation is important; they
have regimentation and their own sub-culture with specific standards,
values and codes of conduct. Nevertheless, it is striking how much the
armed forces display characteristics typical of Dutch society in general
— possibly more so than in other countries, but unfortunately I cannot
speak with full knowledge about this. In many respects the hierarchy in
the armed forces is a reflection of social hierarchy, perhaps more
strictly institutionalised: officers belong to the upper class; the crew
were, for a long time 'the dregs of society'.

Furthermore, it is possible to observe the Dutch *verzuiling*
(pillarization), the denominational and ideological segmentation of Dutch
Society in the armed forces, in spite of the armed forces being a national
organisation. In the reception of soldiers after duty-hours, in spiritual
care and in social activities, one can see this pillarized structure,
especially in the twentieth century. The denominational groups
particularly were and are very active: quite a system of fleet and army
chaplains, numerous Roman Catholic and Protestant servicemen's
recreation centres, and so on. But there was also the social-democratic
branch: a number of unions for lower ranks were more or less openly
social-democratically orientated from the beginning of this century
onwards. And in 1939 social-democratic mobilisation clubs were introduced alongside the Roman Catholic, the Protestant and the general ones.

Developments in labour relations in the armed forces also reflect in
many respects developments in society in general, particularly when we
look at large organisations. About the end of the nineteenth century and
the beginning of the twentieth century associations for the protection of
the interest of professional servicemen were formed. Even if these were
not officially called trade-unions, they can be compared with them,
particularly the associations for the lower rank servicemen. Of course
this was met with opposition. Even more than in society in general it
could be argued that in the armed forces such a thing as a trade-union
was incompatible with the particular nature of the military profession.
It could arguably interfere with the exercise of the military function just
at the time when under extreme conditions it might be required to act.
In the early thirties a change set in, when in 1933 the mutiny on the
armoured vessel *De Zeven Provinciën* seemed to prove the fundamental
flaw in the developments of previous decades. A series of measures
were taken. For example, associations of personnel were limited in their
scope (and some of them disappeared altogether); discipline was

intensified; recruitment was tightened, and so on.[23] Yet in the long term this could not stop the development of a system for protecting the common interest of servicemen in the armed forces. More and more the forces came to be organised along the lines of a modern large-scale enterprise, with the up-to-date methods of personnel management that go along with it. This involves, for instance, a complicated consultative structure at many levels in which protection of interest by the trade-unions has become a common element. Bureaucracy in the armed forces is connected with this. The youngest shoot from the tree of protection of interest — the trade-union of conscripts — has, after a period of searching and exploration, and also after the inevitable conflicts, attended with publicity, more or less found its place.[24] I think that these examples of the penetration of societal developments in the armed forces — and one could add, for instance, the introduction of women into the armed forces — can be seen as aspects of a wider process in which civilian elements became more and more prominent in the armed forces.[25] In the opinion of an ever increasing number of groups and individuals, within as well as outside the services, the armed forces have a specific task. Consequently the organisation will have certain characteristics of its own; but it is more important that they are purposeful, in the same way as other purposeful organisations are.

Therefore the armed forces ought to meet the demands which are required from all sorts of similar organisations, especially government institutions. It can obviously be assumed that, the stronger the position of the armed forces in society, the stronger the emphasis on the particular nature of this organisation can be sustained. Therefore it is not surprising that the civilian approach to the armed forces, which develops in most countries, has been pushed somewhat farther in the Netherlands. At any rate, that is how I feel about it. In this process, in which the armed forces have become more 'civilian', a shift sets in from emphasis on the general military element, with its orientation on the nation, to emphasis on the *professional* element. Servicemen were and are becoming increasingly highly trained specialists in a technical and often very advanced company. Fulfilling such tasks competently and efficiently provides the serviceman with a highly specialised occupation, as well as giving him the opportunity of considerable job satisfaction.

The awareness of working by society's order, in the same way as other people fulfil different tasks, is not necessarily lost. On the contrary, it is the only justification and the only means of achieving social esteem. After all, it is servicemen who are prepared to take up this task of using military force, which is by many considered disagreeable, though they do so in the hope that it will never be necessary to deploy military resources aggressively.

As the armed forces experience social influences in various ways, and are themselves in a sense the result of numerous social and political forces, so those same armed forces are a factor in the social and political order. The question of how much influence they have can only be answered very roughly and subjectively, like many other questions in this chapter. Two remarks can be made with certainty. Policy has clearly established the position of the armed forces, i.e., subordinate to the political institution; and the Dutch armed forces have never seriously disputed this position. *Coups d'états* or serious attempts were absolutely out of the question. There were indeed short periods in or around the two World Wars, during which the Dutch military were in supreme command of the whole country, or parts of it, but then they were always legally entitled to command, but they were ultimately responsible to the political authorities. Het *Militair Gezag* (Military Authority) which played an important role at the end of the Second World War is the most important and well-known example. Though some people thought this Military Authority was occasionally pushed too far, it is a very good illustration of what I have just stated: it was officially instituted and legalised by the government; it was meant to be temporary, and the military never attempted to come into power for a lengthy period.

In fact the reverse happened now and again. Occasionally the government used the armed forces for purposes other than safeguarding the country against external attack. In a way that same Military Authority is an example of such use. More basic examples are the use of the armed forces in riots, kidnappings or hijackings. Whenever assistance in the event of natural disasters was required, the use of the military was undisputed, and this also applied to the deployment of troops in cases of hijackings. In principle this was hardly disputed either, though some people did have practical objections. More difficulties were encountered when troops were brought into action during social conflicts. This happened, or was at least seriously considered, in the case of the second railway strike in 1903, the *Jordaan* riot in 1934 and the suppressing of social unrest immediately after the Second World War and in the sixties and seventies. Overall the government acted very carefully. The action of servicemen was very limited, being usually limited to support of the police forces by contingents of military police or other troops. Anyway, committing servicemen to dealing with social unrest implied and implies a certain risk, at least theoretically, for the same unrest might transfer its effect to the armed forces themselves. The government were apprehensive of this when there was a threat of a social and political revolution in the Netherlands in November 1918. Unrest inside an army camp had been one of the first signs! In the week during which the tension reached its highest point, the Naval Staff even started to disarm the fleet.[26] The mutiny on the *De Zeven Provinciën* in 1933, previously mentioned, gave rise to doubts about the reliability of the armed forces as well. Yet, looking at the twentieth century as a whole, there is no reason to suppose that the armed forces have ever been a serious revolutionary threat. Nor could there be found a serious threat of a *coup d'état* led by the right-wing officers. In short, the armed forces or groups from the armed forces were of little political importance. For a long time for instance, Ministers of War, Navy, or Defence came traditionally from military circles. But this was mainly done for practical reasons. They were supposed to be the experts. However, their actions were not always very successful. The majority of them had a poor command of political skills. When, about 1930, a change took place — from then onwards the majority of defence ministers have been civilians — they operated all in all more successfully. Now and again former servicemen became members of parliament, but their number was never large and they never formed a united front in promoting military interests. Two former servicemen rose to the office of Prime Minister: H. Colijn and P. J. S. de Jong. They were quite successful in their positions, but they certainly did not function as exponents of militarism. So, once again, the armed forces cannot be seen as an important factor in politics. This is not surprising given the historical place of the armed forces in society, which is the result of historical factors and the process of an increasing civilian approach.

Finally, a few words about the present. Historians are generally wise enough to keep their distance from the present, because they do not have a firm foothold there. But in this chapter I have already given so many impressions without that foothold that I dare to stretch my recklessness into the present. I think that modern attitudes towards defence and the armed forces are chiefly set by three factors, each connected to a historical development. In the first place the horrors of war received strong reinforcement during earlier decades. The horrors of the two World Wars play a part in it as proofs from reality, but to me, the potential horrors of a nuclear war seem more effective. These sentiments join with older, sometimes slumbering traditions, which never had the upper hand, but which did exist: sentiments of anti-militarism, peace-mindedness and aversion to the military as a wasteful organisation. Recently these sentiments have led to well organised and very emotional protest-movements and demonstrations focused on concrete issues. But fundamental differences and changes of attitude in the population as a whole did not result from them. There was and is a prevailing non-military attitude.

A second important factor lies in the field of foreign policy. The choice of a national defence under the terms of the Atlantic Alliance, and more generally the choice of the miscellaneous western alliance was a very fundamental one. However confusing the problematical part of this co-operation, and the overrunning of democratic idealism by interests and power-politics may sometimes be, the Netherlands, i.e., the government, parliament and public opinion, has never tampered with this choice since it was firmly established by the Cold War. This choice was of invaluable positive interest for the armed forces. Not only was the necessity for the forces clearer than before, but also the element of uselessness of the Dutch armed forces in case of a real confrontation disappeared from the debates. The doubts which had sometimes been spread by this perspective were replaced by the conviction that defence expenditure contributed to the combined allied defence of what was solemnly called 'the freedom of the West'. Besides, the international contacts formed an inspiration for servicemen personally and for the armed forces as a whole. Especially in these new relations it was possible to achieve highly competent performances.

Thirdly, what I called the process of an increasing civilian approach in the armed forces is important, which is the result of the bureaucrat-isation of the military process and the fact that technology was becoming more and more important. On the other hand it was also connected with the way in which the relations between the armed forces and society developed. As servicemen were able to show more clearly that they from the Netherlands could contribute equally to an internationally necessary task, more appreciation could be displayed in society. Of course this has nothing to do with military heroism and its possible attraction, which was traditionally not very great in the Netherlands, but rather with appreciation for a professional highly qualified job.

In short, the conclusions are: In the Netherlands, war, and thus the armed forces, were and are, generally speaking, increasingly regarded as an evil. But in an imperfect world, in which so much evil exists, the armed forces were and are more and more looked upon as a necessity, as a safeguard against an even greater evil. In my opinion, short-term fluctuations in the course of Dutch history in the twentieth century have not altered this. The characteristic position of the armed forces in twentieth century Dutch society is therefore quite obvious, though not very original — a necessary evil.

Acknowledgements

The author wishes to express his gratitude to K. Treurniet, a student of history at the University of Amsterdam, who, as a trainee of the *Stichting Maatschappij en Krijgsmacht* (Armed Forces and Society Foundation, The Hague) collected most of the material for this chapter. The chapter was translated by Mrs M. C. F. van Drunen and Mrs M. H. van Poelijk.

NOTES

1. As a result of the very broad range of this chapter most of the facts mentioned are well known. Therefore the annotation is limited to quotations and to some more specialised publications.
2. P. J. Blok, *Geschiedenis van het Nederlandsche volk* III (Leiden, 1925), 3rd edn., p. 147.
3. P. J. Blok, *Geschiedenis van het Nederlandsche volk* II (Leiden, 1924), 3rd edn., p. 541.
4. A. J. C. Rüter, 'De Nederlandse natie en het Nederlandse volkskarakter', reprinted in A. J. C. Rüter, *Historische studies over mens en samenleving* (Assen, 1967), p. 314.
5. C. M. Schulten, quoted in *Maatschappelijke waardering voor het militaire beroep*, report of the *Maatschappelijke Raad voor de Krijgsmacht* (Social Council for the Armed Forces) (The Hague, 1987), p. 10.
6. For the thirties of this century there is a collection of essays edited by G. Teitler, *Tussen crisis en oorlog. Maatschappij en krijgsmacht in de jaren '30* (Dieren, 1984). Interesting research is nowadays carried out by the *sectie Militaire Geschiedenis van de Landmachtstaf* (Military History Section of the Army), the *afdeling Maritieme Historie van de Marinestaf* (Historical Department of the Navy) and the *Stichting Maatschappij en Krijgsmacht*. In the near future important books will be published.
7. Ph. P. Everts, *Public opinion, the churches and foreign policies. Studies of domestic factors in the making of Dutch foreign policy* (Leiden, 1983).
8. The results of these research projects are summarised in *Maatschappelijke waardering voor het militaire beroep* (see note 5), pp. 15–17, 59–63.
9. H. Amersfoort, 'Voor Vaderland en Oranje', *Mededelingen van de Sectie Militaire Geschiedenis Landmachtstaf*, 7 (1984), pp. 5–35.

10. F. C. Spits, 'Problems of Defence in a Non-Belligerent Society: Military Service in the Netherlands during the Second Half of the Nineteenth Century', in A. C. Duke and C. A. Tamse, eds, *War and Society, Britain and the Netherlands VI.* (The Hague, 1977), pp. 189–202.

11. According to W. Bevaart, who is working on a Ph.D. thesis about Dutch defence policy 1840–74, the turning point was in 1859 (crisis in Italy).

12. *Handelingen der Tweede Kamer der Staten-Generaal* (Parliamentary Papers) 1897–98, p. 863.

13. J. C. Boogman, 'Die holländische Tradition in der niederländische Geschichte' in J. C. Boogman, *Van spel en spelers. Verspreide opstellen* (The Hague, 1982), pp. 147–61.

14. Quoted by H. J. G. Beunders, *Weg met de Vlootwet! De maritieme bewapeningspolitiek van het kabinet-Ruys de Beerenbrouck en het succesvolle verzet daartegen in 1923* (Amsterdam, 1984), p. 7.

15. A. Doedens, *Nederland en de Frans-Duitse oorlog. Enige aspecten van de buitenlandse politiek en de binnenlandse verhoudingen van ons land omstreeks het jaar 1870* (Zeist, 1973). W. Klinkert is working on a Ph.D. thesis on Dutch defence policy in the last decennia of the nineteenth century. His book, and that of Bevaart (see note 11) will contain very interesting material on this debate.

16. *Handelingen* 1910–11, pp. 1133–34.

17. L. de Jong, *Het Koninkrijk der Nederlanden gedurende de Tweede Wereldoorlog I* (The Hague, 1969), p. 632.

18. Quoted by Beunders, *op. cit.*, p. 110.

19. *Handelingen* 1938–39, p. 465.

20. J. C. H. Blom, 'Durch kamen sie doch. Het Nederlands defensiebeleid in de jaren dertig opnieuw beschouwd', in *Tussen crisis en oorlog* (see note 6), pp. 116–43.

21. Information given by W. Klinkert (see note 15).

22. J. G. Siccama, 'De defensie begroting tussen 1945 en nu, de moeilijk te bepalen prijs van de Nederlandse defensie' in *De prijs van defensie. Produkt van een politieke afweging*, Stichting Maatschappij en Krijgsmacht (The Hague, 1983).

23. J. C. H. Blom, *De muiterij op De Zeven Provinciën. Reacties en gevolgen in Nederland* (Utrecht, 1983), 2nd edn.

24. G. Teitler, 'Conscript unionism in the Dutch army' in G. Harries-Jenkins and J. A. A. van Doorn, eds, *The military and the problem of legitimacy* (London, 1976), pp. 193–213; G. Teitler, 'The successful case of military unionization in the Netherlands' in *Armed Forces and Society*, 2 (1976), pp. 517–28; F. Th. Olivier and G. Teitler, 'Democracy and the Armed Forces; the Dutch "experiment"', in G. Harries-Jenkins, ed., *Armed Forces and the Welfare Societies. Challenges in the 1980s* (London and Basingstoke, 1982), pp. 54–95.

25. See notes 8 and 24.

26. H. J. Scheffer, *November 1918. Journaal van een revolutie die niet doorging* (Amsterdam/Dieren, 1985), especially pp. 173–4.

7

THE ARMED FORCES AND SOCIETY IN BRITAIN

E. J. Grove

Great Britain is an island, and this has inevitably meant that the 'Senior Service' is the Royal Navy. Britons are sometimes surprised to find that they still possess Europe's most powerful navy, but, on second thoughts, it does not seem so unnatural. In the 1980s the Falklands War did a great deal to re-legitimise Britain's naval capabilities in the eyes of the public, as well as to increase the confidence of the armed services in general in the robustness of popular support for their activities. For the Falklands was a classic colonial war of the old type; short, distant and decisive, and the distance emphasised one of the important reasons why the armed services in general and the navy in particular are not seen as a problem: they have tended to operate in areas far from home. They have thus not been a threat to domestic liberties. It is perhaps significant that on one of the few occasions in its history when the Navy was in a position to pose a revolutionary threat — the Nore Mutiny of 1797 — the reaction of the authorities was severe.

The army, however, has been more important than most people think. The only major war in the last three hundred years that Britain lost, the War of American Independence, was lost not only because they were stupid enough to be fighting their most difficult opponents, the Dutch, but also because their enemies were not distracted by a British army on the Continent. Janus-like therefore, Britain in all her successful wars had to face both ways, towards the oceans and towards the Continent. In fact the needs of colonial policing as well as continental commitments meant that Britain usually spent more on her army than on her navy, and the advent of air power complicated this dilemma further. Once the Germans in 1917 had demonstrated the disturbing capability to fly over Britain's traditional 'moat', the British adopted a radical solution. They set up the first independent air force to defend the British Isles through a combination of deterrence and defence.

Creating a third service set an example to the rest of the world, but it also created some problems, notably in the provision of air power at sea. The Royal Navy had to fight a twenty-year battle to assert its right to deploy a Fleet Air Arm, for which it was itself responsible, but the Royal Air Force's concession on this issue was itself a reflection of the growing self-confidence of the junior service: allowing the Navy its own aircraft was not a first step towards partition. The war that came almost immediately after gave the Royal Air Force the opportunity to confirm its status and independence by providing the key element that held off the Germans in 1940. This, much more than the controversial strategic bombing offensive, has provided the popular and positive image of the RAF in the eyes of the British people at large. There has been no serious question of abolishing the RAF even when it lost its core strategic bombing task to the Royal Navy in the 1960s. Instead the RAF was allowed to assert a monopoly of tactical air power at the expense of the Navy's carrier programme. The upgrading of Britain's air defences over the last decade has seen the RAF re-emphasise its most distinctive and publicly acceptable role.

Historically the army in Britain has always been tainted by the Cromwellian experience.[1] That military régime, however, deployed the best army and navy that Britain was to have for many years afterwards. Samuel Pepys struggled to maintain the efficiency of the fleet in the less favourable conditions of the Restoration. He has gone down in popular history as a hero, although his efforts were not so appreciated at the time. Maintaining the navy, however, was, in the last analysis, in the interests even of the King's enemies. James II's efforts to build up a royal army clearly had a more sinister ring and they led directly to his overthrow in the events we celebrated in 1988. The new régime could hardly dispense with land forces, but the famous Mutiny Act passed every subsequent year by Parliament, both made clear who was in control, and that the army was a necessary evil, only to be tolerated on a short-term basis. The army was held in low esteem for many years, only being rehabilitated in the last quarter of the nineteenth century.

Ned Willmott has suggested several reasons why this occurred:[2] the removal of the army from the task of maintaining public order, the ending of billetting with the construction of barracks and military towns, the ending of the practice of using the army as an alternative to prison as a form of penal servitude, the institution of medals and awards for ordinary soldiers, a series of successful colonial wars that received coverage in the first mass circulation newspapers, the abolition of purchase after 1870 and the non-introduction of conscription. The last two deserve special mention. The system of buying commissions was an important way of ensuring that the traditional British ruling class maintained control of the army. Social change, however, was broadening that class and creating new standards of professionalism from which it would have been unwise for reasons of image as well as efficiency to have kept the army insulated. The new middle classes began to regard the army as a respectable profession which their sons could enter.

The lack of conscription is one of the most distinctive features of the British military tradition. Compulsory service was regarded as a fundamentally alien thing, even for the Royal Navy. Although the Tudor state listed mariners for conscription into the Navy, a system that worked effectively in 1588, it was replaced by the infamous press gang, whose arbitrary and unfair features were regarded as more consonant with the liberties of Englishmen than the fairer but more rigorous French form of *Inscription Maritime*. Britain even tried to fight a twentieth-century land war using voluntary enlistment alone, and the raising of Kitchener's Army must go down as one of the most remarkable achievements of the British volunteer tradition. It could not last, but Britain's brief experience with conscription in the last two years of the First World War did nothing to enhance the army's reputation, especially as it was combined with the inevitable losses of even a victorious major war. One of the real ironies of British military history is that perhaps the British army's finest hour, its defeat of the German army in 1918, the only major British victory over a first-rank European military power in modern history, is not regarded with the pride it deserves.[3] Popular memory, even inside the services, dwells on the apparent waste and futility of the Somme and Passchendaele.

After 1918 the natural desire that never again would so many British lives be sacrificed led to much writing about a 'British Way of War' that emphasised maritime strategy, limited liability and the indirect approach. The British army thankfully returned to 'real soldiering' in 1918 and the determination never to go back to the Western Front did much to inhibit its doctrinal and technical development. In the 1930s rearmament priorities emphasised air and sea forces, and only after 1942 did the British army begin to approach the quality of the Germans. Conscription had been reintroduced even before the war in 1939 as the European crisis deepened, and, remarkably, it was continued for a decade and a half after 1945 as Britain was faced with the demands of garrisoning an unstable post-war world without the resources of a diminishing empire. National Service was, however, politically unpopular and widely regarded as economically debilitating in full employment post-war Britain, and the advent of thermonuclear weapons provided a strategic justification for its abolition, announced in the Duncan Sandys White Paper of 1957.

Although public opinion tends to favour the general concept of some form of national service, a reintroduction of conscription is not on the political agenda in the United Kingdom. The armed services are firmly against it as they prefer the inherent efficiency of an all-regular force to the problems of training possibly reluctant conscripts and only getting a limited return of service for the investment.

The armed forces therefore are an even more 'exceptional' element in Great Britain than they are in the Netherlands. They are integrated in Britain's society mainly through Huntingtonian concepts of 'professionalism' and 'objective civilian control'.[4] The armed services are the apolitical servants of whichever government the electoral system produces. Like all crown servants, members of the armed services are not allowed to play an active part in political life. The idea of officers being identified with one political party or another, a commonplace in the Netherlands or in the German Federal Republic, seems very strange. This does, however, have some questionable effects. Not only does it militate against an informed debate on defence and the armed services, but it also tends to encourage a feeling that the natural place for a member of the armed services is on the right of the political spectrum.

More 'subjectively' in Huntingtonian terms,[5] Britain's armed forces are integrated into society at large by being part of the 'establishment' with strong royal connections and the identification (and in the case of certain army regiments integration) of their officers with what might crudely be termed the 'social élite'. One of the remarkable features of the British ruling classes throughout history has been their permeability and willingness to recruit new members. The armed forces have been particularly effective in doing this and their officer training establishments do a most effective job in socialising young men and women of different backgrounds into 'élite' culture and attitudes.

Another form of social integration is the strong regional connections inherent in the army's regimental system since the Cardwell reforms, introduced in 1882. This has been most successful in identifying different parts of the country with their particular units, and it helps create a certain cultural homogeneity within the different regiments. The costs and benefits of the regimental system are a matter of perennial debate, but there can be little doubt that the 'family' feeling engendered does have positive effects on unit cohesion and effectiveness.

The lack of that close integration with outside society that conscription would tend to bring means that the armed forces do not have to respond to the pressures which exist in outside society. For example, women have a much more restricted role in the British armed forces than they have in those of the Netherlands. Progress in providing opportunities for British servicewomen to go into combat or serve at sea is likely to be slow. Similarly, there is no pressure for military trade unionisation of the Northern European type which is regarded with puzzled curiosity by British servicemen. Officers are expected to look after the interests of their subordinates in the best traditions of *noblesse oblige*. The record of officer–man relations is indeed quite good in the British armed services, although there have been occasional break-downs. As Carew has pointed out[6] the Royal Navy's record in the early years of this century was far from sound, and this culminated in the mutiny at Invergordon in 1931, an event which might be instructively compared with the mutiny in the *De Zeven Provinciën* two years later. Invergordon caused a reaffirmation of traditional leadership style, however. Indeed the opportunity was taken to reverse tendencies towards any collective organisation to express sailors' grievances.

The armed forces take their apolitical status very seriously. The fact that the most serious approach to a coup this century was the Curragh Mutiny of 1914 is an index of how little military intervention in politics is even thought about. The fact that it occurred in Ireland is no coincidence, as it has been here that the Government has had to continue to rely upon the armed forces in an internal security role. In Great Britain short historical memories are encouraged to emphasise the exceptional nature of the use of the armed forces as 'aid to the civil power'. This normally takes the form of troops clearing dustbins or providing emergency services rather than maintaining public order. The last time a rioter was shot by a soldier in Great Britain was 1919. This lack of involvement of the armed forces in domestic affairs confirms their status as 'above politics'.

As a result, the armed forces, rather like the monarchy, are held in high regard by the British people. Investigations into popular attitudes to the armed forces have clearly demonstrated their strongly supportive nature.[7] This is partly due to a sense of pride in achievement. The British do not dwell on their defeats; indeed the successful Dutch invasion of 1688 is not seen as an invasion at all. Far from being a military failure it is a matter for mutual celebration. As stated at the outset, the Falklands War confirmed this generally 'triumphalist' popular view of Britain's national naval and military past. British soldiers and sailors win their battles in the popular mind, at least the last ones. Receding negative memories of the 'bull' of conscription are far outweighed by images of military efficiency and effectiveness.

There is therefore quite a strong pro-defence consensus in the United Kingdom which has survived the growth of the anti-nuclear protest movement of the early 1980s.[8] This caused the main opposition party to espouse policies of unilateral nuclear disarmament, but this was a major contributory factor in their electoral unpopularity. No political party pledged to such policies is electable in the United Kingdom, especially as the British argument has tended to revolve around the British national deterrent rather than American cruise missiles. The former is much more popular than the latter. In its propaganda the Government successfully used the Labour Party's approach to nuclear weapons to symbolise an apparent lack of commitment to the defence of the realm. It was hard for the opposition to produce a counter to this, although Labour's commitment to increasing conventional forces did in itself demonstrate the need to reflect the pro-defence feelings of the electorate.

It is hard for Labour to shake off the image of being 'unsound' on defence, although post-war Labour Governments have never shirked their defence responsibilities. Indeed, it is not too far from the truth to sum up the record of post-1945 governments as the Conservatives saying they would spend more on defence, but actually spending less, and the Labour Party saying they would spend less, but actually spending more. Governments of both parties have had to respond to the electorate's domestic investment priorities; health, welfare and education before defence, but both parties have had to reflect the pro-defence consensus also. Since 1945 the proportion of British gross domestic product spent on defence has always been the highest in Europe, leaving aside the special cases of Greece and Turkey. In 1985 the figure stood at 5.2 per cent compared to the 3.1 per cent for the Netherlands.[9]

The British people do not have a 'small country' mentality. They expect their forces to be large and relatively well equipped. They are not so internationalist as the Dutch, who took the lead in creating the European dimension for the naval presence in the Gulf, something which future historians may well call one of the most significant events in the creation of a European defence identity. Such a framework was not necessary in the United Kingdom to legitimise the Armilla Patrol. But, despite its enthusiasm for national military activities, Britain is not a 'militarist' country in any of the possible meanings of the word.[10] As we have seen, it is not militocratic or militarised.[11] Its people's pride in the armed services, and slightly unhealthy fixation with the Second World War, fall short of 'militolotary'.[12] Nevertheless, there is a strong pro-defence consensus in the country that fosters a healthy relationship with the traditionally organised and run armed services. Like many things British, the relationship of the United Kingdom's armed forces with society at large is idiosyncratic and distinctive. But it seems to work rather well.

NOTES

1. The classic study is C. H. Firth, *Cromwell's Army* (London, 1902).
2. In an unpublished paper prepared in 1988 and kindly made available to the author when preparing these remarks.
3. See the various works of John Terraine which emphasise the British Army's World War I achievements. Although Terraine's work is open to criticism it is a most useful antidote to the 'lions led by donkeys' analysis of British military leadership in the First World War found in most other authors.
4. S. P. Huntington, *The Soldier and the State: The Theory and Politics of Civil-Military Relations*, (Cambridge, Mass., 1957), pp. 30-9, 80-5.
5. *Ibid.*, 80-3.
6. A. Carew, *The Lower Deck of the Royal Navy 1900-1935: Invergordon in Perspective* (Manchester, 1981).
7. D. Capitanchik, 'Public Opinion and Popular Attitudes Towards Defence', in J. Baylis, ed., *British Defence Policy in a Changing World* (London, 1977).
8. D. Capitanchik, *The Changing Attitude to Defence in Britain*, Centrepiece 2 (Aberdeen, 1982) provides an interesting perspective from the time when the debate was at its height. He was able to argue that 'historically Britain does *not* have a pacifist tradition; and even the possession of nuclear weapons has always been supported by a majority of the population', p. 42.
9. *The Military Balance 1988-89* (International Institute for Strategic Studies, London), p. 224.
10. S. Andreski, *Military Organisation and Society*, 2nd edn (London, 1968), pp. 184-6.

11. 'Militocracy' = preponderance of the military over the civil; 'Militarization'
    = the extensive control of the military over social life, coupled with the
    subservience of the whole society to the needs of the army. Andreski, *Ibid.*,
    pp. 184–5.
12. Defined as 'adulation of the military virtues', *Ibid.*, p. 186.

INDEX

Note: Persons, ships and geographical names are included

Aberdeen, G. Hamilton-Gordon, 4th
    Earl of 62, 63, 65
Aceh 59, 62, 85
Aerssen, F. van 20, 26
Albemarle, W. A. van Keppel, 2nd
    Earl of 24
Almonde, Ph. van 15–17
Amboina 73
Amersfoort, H. 89
Amparán, Don M. d', 50
Amsterdam 2, 3, 7, 9, 15, 16, 24, 25,
    91
Anjou, Philip of, see Philip V
Anne of Hanover 43
Antilles
Antwerp 39
Argo 5
Athlone, G. van Reede van Ginkel,
    1st Earl of 38
Auchmuty, Sir S. 56
Auerquerque, see Nassau-Ouwerkerk
Augsburg 35
Australia 64
Austria 42, 44, 46, 76
Austrian Netherlands, see Southern
    Netherlands
Ayscue, Sir G. 86

Bachrach, A. G. J. v
Baer van Slangenburg, F. J. van
    38–40
Balchen, Sir J. 20
Bali 58, 64, 65
Ball, A. 52
Baltic 5, 6, 8, 16, 18, 84
Bandung 60
Banjarmasin 56
Barcelona 49
Barfleur 13

Bathurst, H. Bathurst, 2nd Earl 26
Batavia 49, 51–55, 60, 73, 76
Baud, J. C. 62, 63
Beachy Head 13
Bedford, J. Russell, 4th Duke of 21,
    23
Belgium (see also Southern
    Netherlands) 35
Bencoolen 58, 59
Bengal 25, 27
Bentinck, C. J. 22
Bentinck, J. B. 24
Bentinck van Rhoon, Count W.
    22–24
Berezina 85
Berkeley, Sir W. 86
Beuningen, C. van 8
Beveziers 13
Biliton 59
Birmingham 62
Black, J. 27
Blok, P. J. 86
Blom, J. C. H. vii, ix, 84
Bonn 38
Boogman, J. C. 91
Booy, A. de 72
Borneo 56, 59, 61, 63–65, 67
Bosch, E. B. van den 57
Bosscher, Ph. M. v, 27
Braam, J. P. van 53
Brooke, J. 61, 63
Bruijn, J. R. v, 3, 27
Brussels 38
Buitenzorg 55
Bylandt, C. M. E. G. Count van 64,
    65

Cadiz 4, 5, 50
Callenburgh, G. 17

113

Calvert, H. 45
Camperdown 51
Cape St. Vincent 20
Cape of Good Hope 27
Cardwell, E. 108
Carew, A. 109
Carter, A. 7
Castlereagh, R. Stewart, styled
　　Viscount (later 2nd Marquess of
　　Londonderry) 58
Ceylon 74
Channel, see English Channel
Charles II, King of England and
　　Scotland 8, 33–35
Charles IV, King of Spain 49
Charles VI, Emperor of Germany 42
Chatham 84
Chesterfield, P. D. Stanhope, 4th
　　Earl of 19
China 59, 73
Churchill, C. 38, 39
Churchill, J., see Marlborough
Churchill, Sir W. S. 41, 71
Coen, Jan Pietersz. 53
Cologne 46
Colijn, H. 70, 71, 95, 101
Cumberland and Brunswick-
　　Luneburg, W. A. Duke of 43
Curaçao 1, 54
Curragh 109

D'Amparán, Don M. 50
D'Anna & Elizabeth 1
Dacres, 54
Daendels, H. W. 55–57, 60
Dartmouth, W. Legge, 1st Earl of 17
Davis, T. 24
De Zeven Provinciën 98, 101, 109
Dedel, S. Baron 62, 64
Den Helder v
Denmark 5, 8, 13
Derby 21
Die Hoffnung 49
Downs 84
Doorman, K. W. F. M. 86
Drevers-Driesen, I. L. vi
Drunen, M. C. F. van iii, 103

Dunkirk 16, 17
Dutch East Indies 49–83, 84, 86
Dyle 38

Ekeren 39
Elout, C. T. 61
English Channel 1, 8, 13, 25, 38, 79
Enkhuizen 2
Esmeralda 49
Evertsen, C. 8, 13
Eyck van Heslinga, E. S. van vii, ix, 1

Falkland Islands 105, 110
Fendall, J. 57
Flanders 34
Flushing 16
Fontenoy 43
France 5, 6, 8, 10, 15, 19, 20, 24,
　　25, 33, 34, 36, 40, 42, 44–46, 77,
　　79, 87, 88
Friderici, J. F. 51
Friesland 2

Genoa 24
Gelderland 38
George I 14, 19
George II 22, 43, 44
George III 25, 44
Germain, G. Germain, styled Lord G.
　　26
Germany 37, 45, 71, 73, 79, 85, 87,
　　88, 93, 108
Gibraltar 16, 84
Ginkel, see Reede van Ginkel
Goeman Borgesius, H. 90
Gold Coast 61
Grave, H. 20, 22
Greece 110
Grove, E. J. v, vii, ix, 105
Guelders (Gelderland) 38

Haarlem 85
Haarlem 23
the Hague 16, 17, 19, 26, 36, 43, 65,
　　75, 76, 90
Halifax, G. Saville, 1st Earl &
　　Marquess of 35

Hampden Trevor, R. 43
Hanover 18, 44
Hanover, Anne of 43
Harlingen 2
Harrington, W. Stanhope, 1st Baron
    (later 1st Earl of Harrington) 19
Hawke, Sir E. 22
Heemskerck, J. van 84
Heiligerlee 85
Heinsius, A. 9, 36
Hellevoetsluis 1, 23, 24
's Hertogenbosch 85
Hille-Kabel, J. G. M. van 10
Hillsborough, W. Hill, 1st Earl of
    (later 1st Marquess of Downshire)
    26
Hofdijk, W. J. 93
Holland (province) 2, 10, 14–17, 19,
    36, 90
Hooft, W. 't 20, 21
Hoorn 2
Hope, I. 1
Hope, Z. 1
Huy 39

India 27, 52, 56, 59, 65
Indonesia (see also Dutch East
    Indies) 35
Invergordon 109
Ireland 8, 13
Irwin, G. 63
Italy 35

Jamaica 1
James II and VII (see also York)
    34–36, 106
Janssens, J. W. 56
Japan 71, 73, 75, 85
Java 49–52, 55–59, 65, 66, 74, 75
Java Sea 86
Johnson, S. 12
Jones, J. P. 25
Jong, P. J. S. de 101
Jonge, J. C. de 4
Jumel 56

Keppel, A. 24
Kew 54
Kinsbergen, J. H. van 5, 6, 26, 27
Kitchener of Khartoum, H. H.
    Kitchener, 1st Earl 107
Knoop, W. J. 35

Labuan 63
Lansberge, J. W. van 61
Leander 79
Leiden 54, 85
Leopold I 36
Liège 38
Lisbon 23
London 14, 16, 21, 54, 58, 59,
    61–64, 66, 71, 80
Louis XIV v, 13, 15, 33–36, 41
Louis Napoleon 55
Louvain 39, 40

MacArthur, D. 74
Madrid 49, 50
Malacca 59
Malaya 73, 74, 76
Mallorca 49, 51
Maria Theresia 23, 42
Marlborough, J. Churchill, 1st Earl
    and Duke of 13, 36–40, 43
Mary II v, 33, 34
Maurice 85, 86
May, J. 24
Mediterranean 6, 8, 15, 16, 20, 49,
    50, 84
Meester Cornelis 55, 56
Middelburg 2, 16, 17
Minto, G. Elliot-Murray-
    Kynynmound, 1st Baron (later 1st
    Earl of Minto) 56
Mitchell, M. 21
Moluccas 53
Monmouth, J. Scott or Stuart, Duke
    of 34
Montagu, see Sandwich
Moor, J. A. de vii, ix, 49
Moorrees, J. W. 55
Morocco 15
Munster 46

Mountbatten, L. F. A. V. N.
Mountbatten, styled Lord Louis
(later 1st Earl Mountbatten of
Burma) 74, 75

Napoleon I 36, 45, 56, 85
Nassau-Ouwerkerk, H. Count of 38,
39
Nassau, William Louis of
New Guinea 78, 80
New Zealand 76
Newcastle, T. Pelham Holles, 1st
Duke of 21
Nieuwpoort 85
Nimwegen 34
Nootka Sound 26
Nore 105
Norris, Sir J. 9, 18
North, F. North, styled Lord (later
8th Earl of Guildford) 26
North Sea v, 6, 8, 57, 76
North Borneo, see Borneo
Norwegian Sea 80
Nottingham, D. Finch, 2nd Earl of
(later Earl of Winchelsea) 13, 17

Obdam, see Wassenaar-Obdam
Ochakov 27
Onrust 52
Ouwerkerk, see Nassau-Ouwerkerk

Pacific 73, 86
Palmerston, H. J. Temple, 3rd
Viscount 65
Paris 35
Passchendaele 107
Paz 49
Pellew, Sir E. 52
Pepys, S. 106
Persian Gulf 110
Philip II 84
Philip V 35
Philippines 73
Pichegru, C. 45
Piepelenbosch, D. vi
Pieterse, K. 1
Pitt, W. (the younger) 27

Poelijk, M. J. van 103
Portsmouth 17, 23
Portugal 6
Prince of Wales 73
Provincie van Utrecht 24
Prud'homme van Reine, R. B. 10
Prussia 19, 42, 44, 46
Punjab 65

Quatre Bras 85

Raders, J. E. van 51
Raffles, T. 56–58
Rangoon 74
Raven, G. J. A. iii, v, vi, ix
Reede van Ginkel, Earl of Athlone,
G. van 38
Repulse 73
Rodger, N. A. M. iii, vi, vii, x, 12
Rooke, Sir G. 16
Rotterdam 1, 2
Russia 5, 45, 85
Rüter, A. J. C. 87
Ruyter, M. A. de 84, 86
Ryswick 35, 36

St. Eustatius 25
Salisbury, R. A. T. Gascoyne-Cecil,
3rd Marquess of 64
Sandwich, J. Montagu, 4th Earl of
21, 26, 43
Sandys, D. 108
Sas, N. C. F. van 57
Saxe, M. Count of 43
Scheldt 21
Schimmelpenninck, G. Count 65
Schotte, A. 53
Schrijver, C. 22, 23, 27
Schulten, C. M. 87
Scotland v, 43
Scott, H. M. 27
Seeley, Sir J. R. 52
Seymour, H. 51
Siak 59
Siborne, W. 35
Siccama, J. G. 97
Sicily 84

Singapore 58, 59, 70, 71, 73, 74, 76
Slangenburg, see Baer van
  Slangenburg
Slingelandt, S. van 20, 24
Soignies, Forest of 39
Somme 107
Sound 5, 9
Soundings 8
Southern Netherlands 35, 37, 40, 42,
  43, 44
Soviet Union 76, 80
Spain 4, 6, 20, 26, 33, 42, 50, 51,
  54, 55, 84
Spanish Netherlands, see Southern
  Netherlands
Speyk, J. C. J. van 85
Spiegel, L. P. van de 45
Spithead 6, 20, 21, 24, 26
Stormont, D. Murray, 7th Viscount
  (later 2nd Earl of Mansfield) 26
Straits of Malacca 59
Stuart, James Edward 36
Suez 78, 80
Sukarno, A. 75
Sumatra 58, 59, 61, 62, 65, 67
Surinam 50, 51, 53, 54, 57
Sweden 5
Swieten, J. van 64
Swift, J. 18
Switzerland 42

Teitler, G. v, vii, x, 70
Texel 25
Thurlow, E. Thurlow, 1st Baron 26
Timor 73
Torbay v
Torrington, A. Herbert, 1st Earl of 13
Toulon 24
Townshend, C. Townshend, 3rd
  Baron (later 3rd Viscount
  Townshend) 20
Treurniet, K. 103
Trevor, R. H. 43
Trincomalee 27
Turkey 110

United States vi, 72, 73, 77, 78, 80
Utrecht 18, 40, 42

Valckenaar, J. 49–54
Verhees-van Meer, J. Th. H. 10
Vernon, E. 21
Verstolk van Soelen, J. G. 60
Veth, L. de 9, 18
Vienna 16, 36, 45
Villeroy, F. de Neufville, Duke of 39,
  40
Voorda, B. 54
Vries, Joh. de 6

Waal, E. de 59
Wade, G. 42
Wager, Sir G. 20
Warnsinck, J. C. M. 4
Washington 80
Wassenaar-Obdam, J. van 38
Waterloo 35, 85
West Africa 61
West Indies 1, 8, 16, 53, 54, 57, 84
Westerdijkshoorn 24
Westminster 33
Whitaker, Sir E. 17
White Sea 6
Wielingen 86
Wilhelmina 89
Willemstad 54
William I, Stadholder 84
William II, Stadholder 14
William III, Stadholder and King v,
  3–5, 8, 12–15, 17, 23, 24, 33–36,
  38, 43, 46
William IV, Stadholder 14, 22, 23, 43
William V, Stadholder 5, 14, 26, 44,
  54
William I, King 60, 92
William Louis of Nassau 85
Willmott, H. P. v, 106
Wishart, Sir J. 17
Wijck, jhr. C. van der 60

York & Albany, James, Duke of (see
  also James II and VII) 33

York & Albany and Brunswick-
    Luneburg, Frederick, Duke of
    (later 2nd Marquess of London-
    derry) 44, 45
Yorke, Sir J. 26
Yssche 38, 39

Zanden, J. L. van 6
Zeeland 2, 8, 10, 16, 21
Zuiderzee 84
Zwitzer, H. L. v, vii, xi, 33